PRIMERS

MW00677092

Touching the City

WILEY

PRIMERS

Touching the City

Thoughts on Urban Scale

TIMOTHY MAKOWER

WILEY

Registered office
John Wiley & Sons Ltd, The Atrium, Southern Gate, Chichester, West Sussex, PO19 8SQ,
United Kingdom

For details of our global editorial offices, for customer services and for information about how
to apply for permission to reuse the copyright material in this book please see our website at
www.wiley.com.

Executive Commissioning Editor: Helen Castle
Production Editor: Tessa Allen
Assistant Editor: Calver Lezama

ISBN 978-1-118-73772-9 (paperback)
ISBN 978-1-118-73758-3 (ebk)
ISBN 978-1-118-73769-9 (ebk)
ISBN 978-1-118-73770-5 (ebk)
ISBN 978-1-118-94769-2 (ebk)

Cover design, page design and layouts by Karen Willcox, karenwillcox.com
Cover image ©Tim Makower
Printed in Italy by Printer Trento Srl

Acknowledgements

It is impossible to put into words my gratitude to Sibella, Noah, Sylvie and Bonnie for the support they have given to this project, and for putting up with me writing while eating porridge at the breakfast table. Graciela Moreno of UCL and Helen Castle of John Wiley & Sons have been central to the work; without them it would not have happened. Also thanks are due to Miriam Murphy, Caroline Ellerby, Calver Lezama and Edward Denison. I would specially like to thank my parents Peter and Katharine, my brother Andrew and his family, Richard and Anne, and Randle and Amanda, Charlotte and Alice Baker Wilbraham and Paul Randour for their cherished encouragement.

Great thanks go to Bob Allies and Graham Morrison for giving me my foundation in architecture and urbanism, and to all those at Allies and Morrison whom I have worked with over the years. I would also like to thank Mike Hussey of Almacantar, Greg Tillotson and Alastair Baird of Barratt London, Roger Madelin and David Partridge of Argent, Shem Krey and Ramez and Motaz Al Khayyat of UrbaCon, Yousef Al Horr of GORD, Saad Al Muhannadi of Qatar Foundation and Issa Al Mohannadi of Qatar Tourism Authority, Alaa Larri and Fatima Fawzi and my other former colleagues at Msheireb Properties, and Bassam al Mannai and Othman Zarzour of the Supreme Committee for Delivery and Legacy.

Many thanks also for support and help from Mohammad Ali Abdullah, Ibtehaj Al Ahmadani, Bez Baik, Ben Barber, Oliver Barratt, Adrian and Vero Biddell, Peter Bishop, Alain de Botton, Claire Bufflier, Ed Carr, Mark Cazalet, Annie Chillingworth, Chris Choa, Alan Cobb, Tom Cornford, Kees Christiaanse, Hina Farooqi, Terry Farrell, Paul Fisher, Simon Gathercole, Clare Gerrard, Daniel and Olivia Gerrard, Kerry Glencorse, Ana Gonzalez, Mariana Heilmann, Jerry Herron, Mark Hewitt, Hendrik Heyns, Niall Hobhouse, Kelly Hutzell, Ibrahim Jaidah, Charles Jencks, Shalini John, Anna Joynt, Crispin Kelly, Sasha and James Kennedy, Chris Lee, Annabel Lord, Donna MacFadyen, James Meek, Chris Millard, James and Mary Miller, Velina Mirincheva, Lucy Mori, Mohsen Mostafavi, Jean Nouvel, Chris Panfil, Tom and Katie Parsons, Fred Pilbrow, Jorn Rabach, Hafid Rakem, John Rose, Martin and Harriet Roth, Fatma Al Sahlawi, Rami al Samahy, Paulo Sousa, Stephen Taylor, Pete Veale, Tim Wells, Oliver Wong and Carter Worth.

Contents

Foreword

Scaling the XXL

The essence of scale is that it is simultaneously finite and infinite. When we observe a building from the perspective of scale, we observe it as it is, embedded in its localised context. But we are also aware of the fact that at the lower end of the scale its details do not end with the doorknob, and that at the upper end of the scale it is part of a neighbourhood, a city, a country and a greater economic and political region.

In architecture and urbanism, scale thus oscillates between the tangible and the material on the one hand and the abstract and the conceptual on the other. Good design reflects this parallel (in-)finite quality, the relation between the scale of observation and the universe, and the relation between the detail and the overarching concept. Bad design is merely S, M, L, XL or even XXL!

Billboard in Chelsea,
New York, 2013
Manhattan vacillates
successfully between
scales like no other city in
the world, with its urban
grid providing an essential
touchstone. Chelsea – once
an industrial area of wharfs,
distilleries and factories – is
now an 'upscale' residential,
retail and gallery district.

Proportion plays a key role in this reciprocal reflection. When, as a continental European, I first saw English and American early 20th-century architecture, I asked myself why is it mediated by such a strong feeling of scale, until I realised that it was designed in feet and inches, whereas continental modernist buildings were designed using millimetres, centimetres and metres, which in its minutiae is proportionally dead. I then understood Le Corbusier's urge to conceive the Modulor.

The awareness of this parallel (in-)finity may also be the reason that most successful urban design projects are designed by architects and not by planners. Urban designers tend to grow out of architects, as their projects become larger and more complex, constantly calibrating their work with multiple scale-levels, from the strategic or tactical and the material to the abstract and conceptual. In this way they can even make their XXL project become tangible at a giant scale, or, as Tim Makower asserts here in his Conclusion, have the potential to bring together 'the notion of the child and the giant in us all'.

Kees Christiaanse

Kees Christiaanse is Chair of Architecture and Urban Design at ETH Zurich and Programme Leader of the Future Cities Laboratory Singapore ETH Centre for Sustainable Development. Previously a Partner at OMA in Rotterdam, Christiaanse founded KCAP Architects&Planners in 1989. KCAP is based in Rotterdam and has two branch offices in Zurich and Shanghai.

Introduction

'No pattern is an isolated entity. Each pattern can exist in the world, only to the extent that it is supported by other patterns: the larger patterns in which it is embedded, the patterns of the same size that surround it, and the smaller patterns which are embedded in it.'

Christopher Alexander, *A Pattern Language*, 1977[1]

London from the air, 2012
Big shapes: river, Roman roads and parks.

Richard Rogers and Renzo Piano, Centre Pompidou and Place Beaubourg, Paris, 1977 (photographed in 2012)
Super-scaled machine meets fine-grain city: a fertile combination.

Allies and Morrison, Diwan Annex, Doha, 2013
Irresistible to touch: drawn by hand, cut by machine.

This book is about scale as it is manifested in cities. The word 'scale' can be defined as the 'experience of size'. The book explores scale in cities, in the spaces between buildings, in buildings themselves and in their details. It seeks to ask how scale in the cities we inhabit can make us feel at home in the world or alien from it; connected or disconnected. Scale in cities is both

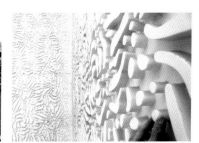

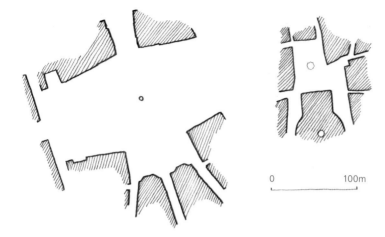

Scale comparison between Piazza della Rotonda and Piazza del Popolo, Rome: drawing by the author, 2014
Rome: a city of intimacy and grandeur.

relative and absolute. 'Getting the scale right' – although it is impossible to define such a thing – is a fundamental part of the magic of architecture and urban design. There are over-sized places, which make people feel small, and there are well-sized places, which can make people feel comfortable, and sometimes larger than life.

Christopher Alexander, in his seminal manifesto on scale and touch, *A Pattern Language*, identifies a problem: 'the languages which people have today are so brutal, and so fragmented, that most people no longer have any language to speak of at all – and what they do have is not based on human or natural considerations'.[2] The beauty of his book, which seeks to address this problem by considering the connection between people and their built environment – the joining together of the fragmented world of experience – is that it connects not just from one thing to another, from outer to inner, but also from macro to micro; it zooms in.

Zooming In

So in what way does scale make a difference? There are the dangers of lumpiness and laziness in design which can arise from working too fast, and there is an economic paradox in the fact that developments which seek to cover too great an area in too little time – notionally benefiting from 'economies of scale' – can destroy their own value by ending up monotonous or characterless. As with cuisine, fast food has its limitations; slow food

is more nutritious and generally more delicious. The same is true of urbanism. These conundrums are worthy of discussion. Of the many aspects of scale to be discussed in this book, two main points stand out. Firstly that scale matters, and is essential to good design and the understanding of cities. Secondly that both big and small are beautiful; both are right, neither is wrong; it all depends on their relationships.

Fast food, London
Not nourishing the body.

The book travels from Detroit via Paris, Doha, New York and other places to London, looking at cities both with the analytical eye of a designer and with the experiential eye of the 'nine- or ninety-year-old'; the person on the street. It looks at old cities and asks what is good about them; what can we learn from the old to inform the new? Like Christopher Alexander's *A Pattern Language*, the book zooms in from the macro scale of surfing Google Earth

Fast urbanism, Doha
Not nourishing the
community.

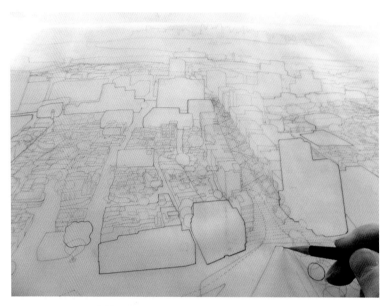

Makower Architects, Al Asmakh, Doha, 2014
The macro-strategy for Al Asmakh is to make the central spine – 'Triple-A Street' – into a linear public space, connecting into the heart of Msheireb, to the north.

Allies and Morrison, Qatar National Archive, Doha, 2011
The carved forms of the project were drawn over by hand, as if being sculpted by the pencil.

to micro moments such as finding fossils in a weathered wall. It examines the dynamics and movement patterns of cities, the making of streets and skylines, the formation of facades, and the honing of thresholds. It also touches on the process of design and the importance of drawing.

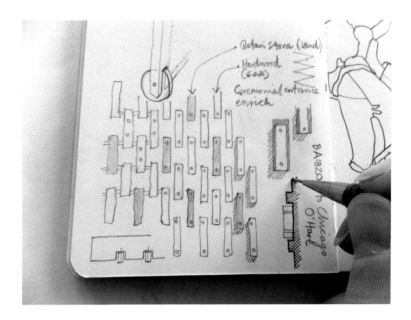

The title – *Touching the City* – reminds us that the city is indeed something physical, and it is alive. We can touch it and it can touch us. Rather than just being in it, we can be of it. To be able to touch a burnished brass door handle at one moment, to enjoy the crank of a wall or the bristling of chimneypots in the next, and to close our eyes, zoom right out and understand the entire shape of a city, both in time and space, is not only essential for a designer; it is valuable for all of us who experience the tactile nature of cities, both actually and metaphorically. The aim of this book is to talk about these things, which are formative in the making and re-making of cities over time, and so to push forward the debate: what place does scale have in the making of good cities for people?

In the early 1970s, when I was six or seven, in the days leading up to Christmas, when we were staying with my grandparents and I was sharing an attic room with my sister, before going to sleep I would describe out loud, into the darkness, models of towns from my imagination, impossibly detailed, all in motion; lights, cars, people; all crystal clear. These were the Christmas presents of my dreams. One of these models was a great city with tall buildings, a huge park and a railway station; another was a harbour town with a long jetty, a marketplace and a domed church; a third was a village on a hill with a castle and a manor house and a bridge across a small river valley.

Eliel Saarinen, Cranbrook
Art Museum, Bloomfield
Hills, Michigan, 1942
The door handle is part of a
solid bronze casting. It brings
together the functional,
aesthetic and tactile
language of the building.

Flying over a town,
somewhere between
Chicago and Kansas City,
2010
The Jefferson Ordnance rides
regardless over a landscape
of hills, rivers and historic
paths; the irregular informs
the regular.

My sister would join in with the descriptions. In the darkness, we felt we could reach out and touch these models but we held off, because they were so fragile. Once I remember thinking I saw an aeroplane fly over one of the models, far below me.

Under the Table

'There is a kind of play common to nearly every child; it is to get under a piece of furniture or some extemporized shelter of his or her own and exclaim that he or she is in a "house".' John Summerson, 'Heavenly Mansions', 1949[3]

John Summerson in his seminal essay 'Heavenly Mansions' describes the child's activity of playing with a doll's house as a 'strict analogy' between the world of the child and that of adulthood. Nothing could be a truer example of this than my own experience with imaginary cities, towns and villages in my grandparents' attic, although seen through the other end of the telescope. Summerson writes of the child playing under a table or with dolls and doll's houses as follows: 'he is placing either himself or the doll (a projection of himself) in a sheltered setting [...] the pleasure he derives from it is a pleasure in the relationship between himself (or the doll) and the setting.'[4]

The table used by the author as a 'house' when he was a child
Sometimes its walls were made of linen sheets, and sometimes of adult legs.

He makes a connection between the 'cosiness' of the little house and the value of 'ceremony', as a signal for inner comfort in a world full of challenges; 'for us the ceremonial idea is more important – the idea of neatness and serenity within, contrasting with wildness and confusion without'. He even refers to camping and sailing as 'adult forms of play analogous to the "my house" pretences of a child. In both there is the fascination of the miniature shelter which excludes the elements by only a narrow margin and intensifies the sense of security in a hostile world.'[5] However he does not mention that the child is seeking to be 'larger than life' (the child wants to grow up). The child in us all, however old we are, is seeking to transcend the everyday tangible world and, as with the large-scale model in the attic, to gain a perspective on life.

My main interest in writing this book is to think about, and to address, people who have not been educated or brainwashed in the subject of architecture or urban design but who are attuned to their environment and who know what they like. The universal relevance of Summerson's point to our relationship with the city is that in all of us there is both a child and a giant. The child, aspiring to adulthood, aggrandises the world through imagination, while the giant, harbouring the infant within, miniaturises in order to gain a 'touch' on the city. The child empathises with the doll who is in turn within the child's realm, but it is not so much a sense of possession or ownership we are concerned with as a sense of belonging.

Intermediary Scale

Summerson goes on to discuss 'aedicules' – the use of miniature structures in the architecture of buildings to break down the scale of the whole into a set of interconnected elements, the entirety of which will amount to something greater, and perhaps grander, than the sum of the parts: 'the aedicule has been used to harmonize architecture of strictly human scale with architecture of a diminutive scale, so that a building may at the same time serve the purposes of men and of a race of imaginary beings smaller than men. It has also been used to preserve the human scale in a building, deliberately enlarged to express the superhuman character of a god [...] enlarged to human scale and then beyond.'[6] I am not alone

Michelangelo, aedicule of St Peter's Basilica, Rome, 1590
The aedicule brings intermediary scale, catering for the giant in us all.

in feeling the resonance of Summerson's analogy. Gerald Adler in his chapter on 'Little Boxes' in his book *Scale: Imagination, Perception and Practice in Architecture*[7] quotes the same opening passage and uses it to examine carefully scaled sequences of space and detail in architecture.

Although Summerson was talking about architecture, a similar point applies to the urban realm. In his thinking, we find that the subject and the object of consideration – both the viewer and the detail, building, space or city which is being viewed – are benefiting from 'intermediary scale': the possibility for mind and body to empathise with things outside themselves and to achieve a state of intimacy or grandeur, beyond what is normal. Intermediary scale in terms of perception is enabling us to experience the largest and smallest of scales in parallel. In terms of our built environment, it is what connects the large and the small in a series of graded and tangible steps.

Leon Battista Alberti, in the first book of his mid-15th-century treatise on architecture, relates the scale of the house to the scale of the city: 'as the philosophers maintain, the city is like some large house and the house is in turn like some small city'.[8] The domestic analogy between the house and the city is relevant in our aim to answer the questions 'What aspects of scale in a city are good for people?' and 'What makes people feel "at home"?' The blurring of boundaries and acknowledgement of overlaps between inner and outer worlds, between private rooms and urban rooms, between large and small scales; this is all part of scaling cities to suit ourselves, who are both the makers and users of the metropolis.

In the book *Powers of Ten: About the Relative Size of Things in the Universe* (1982) by Philip and Phylis Morrison and the Office of Charles and Ray Eames, the notion of approximate absolutes is suggested as a way for us to 'gauge' our environment: 'The world at arm's length – roughly one meter in scale – is the world of most artifacts […] six orders of magnitude cover the entire domain of familiarity'.[9] The book is a systematic examination of a series of images taken at 42 decreasing powers of ten; zooming in from the Cosmos to the atom. With an emphasis on approximation it suggests that there are normative scales to which all things in the world around us relate and, with our own normative dimensions of average height, arm's length, span and pace, it examines how we relate to them. This becomes a framework of approximate norms which enables us to discern, or at least to discuss, how scale-ratios – a journey through a city, the width or unbroken length of a street, the height-to-breadth ratio of a public space, the articulation of the

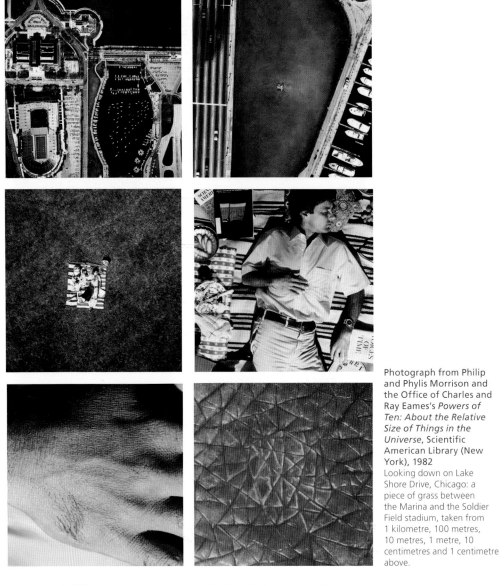

Photograph from Philip and Phylis Morrison and the Office of Charles and Ray Eames's *Powers of Ten: About the Relative Size of Things in the Universe*, Scientific American Library (New York), 1982
Looking down on Lake Shore Drive, Chicago: a piece of grass between the Marina and the Soldier Field stadium, taken from 1 kilometre, 100 metres, 10 metres, 1 metre, 10 centimetres and 1 centimetre above.

facade of a building – can work for us practically, socially, aesthetically and emotionally. It is useful, if not to set absolutes for ourselves (since everything is relative) then at least to believe in norms to which we can point or gravitate.

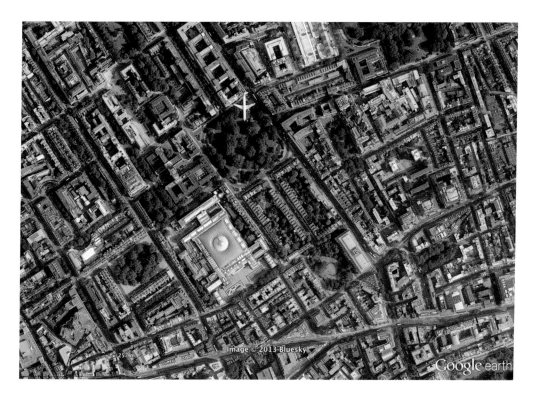

Image © 2013 Bluesky
Google earth

Plane flying over Russell
Square, London
Compression in time and
space.

To Connect or Dis-connect

Today I regularly use Google Earth to explore places I know (and those I
don't) from above. If I zoom in on Russell Square, just north of the British
Museum, to my surprise there is an aeroplane flying due south. The plane
is a flattened white shape; it is impossible to know the distance between it
and the city below. The image was taken on 27 June 2010, and judging by
the shadows, at around nine o'clock in the morning. Who was on the plane?
Someone in a window seat would have been looking down; someone on
the street looking up. Like all photographs, it represents a frozen moment;
but, with Google Earth and the infinite accessibility of information (and to a
degree sensation too) which we have become accustomed to over the last
decade, the image is striking as a compression of simultaneous elements – a
range of scales compounded in time and space. Google Earth has opened
up new horizons for me. Like a child, I feel as if the city is in my hand. The
challenge of course, in EM Forster's lasting words from *Howard's End*, is to

'Only connect [...] Live in fragments no longer'.[10] Nowadays it may be that the wonders of Google Earth and all the other fast-moving, instant-access digital experiences we have come to take for granted engender a sense of scalelessness, making it harder and harder to connect, easier and easier to skate over the surface and not to get involved.

We can understand nothing fully if we do not zoom in and zoom out in parallel, with our eyes and ears wide open and our fingers reaching out to touch. My aim within the pages of this book is to travel this distance. The subject of the book is our ability to connect with the city to the full, aided by a well-judged use of scale in the hands of designers. These things will remain unconscious for most of us, most of the time, but there is value in thinking about them. As the Morrisons and the Eameses wrote:

> 'The Greeks [...] had the idea that deep down below the size we perceive, matter was a web of small modules [...] whose incessant rearrangements account for all becomings. That profound idea [...] has teased out the linked fabric of every substance old and new. It has led to today's view of atomic matter, made clear in the images we build in the land of the small [...] it is related to the world of familiar experience through that same curious blend of the marvelous and the homely that we find out there among the planets.'[11]

References

1 Christopher Alexander, Sara Ishikawa, Murray Silverstein, Max Jacobson, Ingrid Fiksdahl-King and Shlomo Angel, *A Pattern Language: Towns, Buildings, Construction*, Oxford University Press (New York), 1977, p xiii.
2 *Ibid*, p xvi.
3 John Summerson, *Heavenly Mansions [and other essays on architecture]* [1949], WW Norton (New York), 1998, p 1.
4 *Ibid*.
5 *Ibid*, p 2.
6 *Ibid*, p 4.
7 Gerald Adler, Timothy Brittain-Catlin and Gordana Fontana-Giusti (eds), *Scale: Imagination, Perception and Practice in Architecture*, Routledge (New York), 2012.
8 Leon Battista Alberti, *On the Art of Building in Ten Books* [*De Re Aedificatoria*, 1452], translated by Joseph Rykwert, Neal Leach and Robert Tavernor, Dover Publications (New York), 1987, Book One, Chapter 9.
9 Philip and Phylis Morrison and the Office of Charles and Ray Eames, *Powers of Ten: About the Relative Size of Things in the Universe*, Scientific American Library (New York), 1982, p 2.
10 'Only connect! That was the whole of her sermon. Only connect the prose and the passion, and both will be exalted, and human love will be seen at its height. Live in fragments no longer. Only connect, and the beast and the monk, robbed of the isolation that is life to either, will die.' Margaret Schlegel thinking, in EM Forster, *Howard's End* [1910], Penguin Classics, (Harmondsworth), 1973, Chapter 22, p 174.
11 Morrison and Eames, *Powers of Ten*, p 5.

1
On Scale and Size

'Dunwich with its towers and many thousand souls, has dissolved into water, sand and thin air.'

WG Sebald, *The Rings of Saturn*, 1995[1]

Cities grow by nature; few are stable, and some shrink. London doubled in size between 1918 and 1939 but shrank from the 1950s to the 1970s. The population of Paris has tripled in the century from 1910 to 2010 while its land area has increased by 25 times. Doha's population has multiplied a hundred-fold in the last 70 years. Rome shrank from a city of over a million 2,000 years ago to a town of a mere six thousand, 500 years later. The small village of Dunwich in East Anglia, which is now famous only for its fish and chips and has a population of 120 souls, was once 'one of the most important ports in Europe in the Middle Ages. There were more than fifty churches, monasteries and convents, and hospitals here; there were shipyards and fortifications and a fisheries and a merchant fleet of eighty vessels; and there were dozens of windmills. All of it has gone under, quite literally, and is now below the sea, beneath alluvial sand and gravel, over an area of two or three square miles.'[2]

This chapter asks two questions, both from the point of view of the few who are designing and the many who are experiencing cities. Firstly, on the assumption that there is no 'right' or 'wrong' answer as to how large a city should be (either its physical area or its population), are there successful

Cecil Lay, *Dunwich, Suffolk, c* 1930
Before the church was consumed by the North Sea.

ways, healthy ways, that it can be structured in relation to its size; to connect its edges to its centre and to enable healthy growth over time and if necessary, healthy shrinkage? The second question relates to human experience – how do we feel about cities? Do they make us feel small, or larger than life? How is the success or stability of a city connected to our own sense of wellbeing? How are the story of a city, its scale and our own sense of belonging to it, intertwined?

Detroit

In the year of 1701 a French explorer named Antoine de la Mothe founded a fort called Pontchartrain at the straits between Lake Erie and Lake St Clair on the American continent. He was a man of pretensions; a self-styled aristocrat who took on the name of Cadillac, even though he had no connection to the golden chateau near Bordeaux, little knowing that it would be one of the great names synonymous with Detroit – Motor City – two and a half centuries later. America was in those days uncharted territory, an empty continent, a land of opportunity; and Cadillac's well-chosen outpost grew into a successful rural town trading in timber, furs and cooking stoves. In 1787, when Thomas Jefferson, the United States Minister to France at the time, instructed the surveyors Meriwether Lewis and William Clark to cast an orthogonal grid across the whole nation, the small city of Detroit was included. Its town plan, which had grown up around Indian trails, following ancient lines of topography, became part of this great democratic continuum. The evenness of the grid, its ability to overlay and absorb the irregularities of the wild landscape, achieved Jefferson's scientific objective to make this large nation manageable; to rationalise and quantify the land; to share out opportunities fairly for settlers to have a slice of the pie and thus to build a stable and confident citizenry with equal access to the plenteous space, available to all.

The Detroit grid: drawing by the author, 2013
The grid of the city fuses with the National Ordnance; they are threaded together by the diagonal avenues.

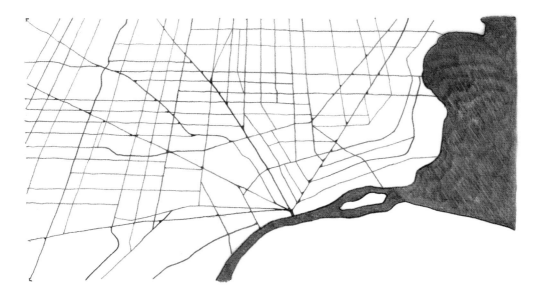

Three centuries later, long after its industrial boom, my own exploration of Detroit found a closeness to untamed nature which I have never known inside a city before, to the point that within minutes of setting out on my first walk, I was physically attacked by a small angry bird, incensed that I was invading his domain.

Centredness

When Judge Augustus B Woodward took pencil to paper in 1805 to masterplan a new Detroit, while the embers of the fire which had destroyed the whole were still smouldering, he was thinking of Washington.[3] I imagine him drawing lines over the map, starting at the centre of the lakeside harbour town and working outwards along the Native American trails of St Anne (now Jefferson) and St Honnerie (now Woodward), creating a radiating plan of diagonals cutting across a grid which ran parallel to the river, showing the influence of the École des Beaux-Arts in Paris. History does not relate whether he ever met Major Pierre L'Enfant, the capital's masterplanner, who said of his plan that it 'should be drawn on such a scale as to leave room for aggrandizement and embellishment which the increase of the wealth of the nation will permit it to pursue at any point, however remote'.[4] However, Woodward emulated the scale and centredness of the Washington Plan, and made sure that it offered plenty of room for growth.

Woodward Avenue, Detroit
The main street of the city runs straight for over 50 kilometres (30 miles), becoming narrower towards the centre of Detroit.

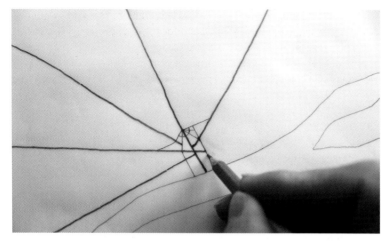

Plan of Detroit, 1805
The bones of the city plan:
grand avenues originating
from Native American trails.

Assuming that his pencil had not been sharpened to a fine point that day,
it might have made a line a millimetre thick; that is about 50 metres (160
feet) at a scale of 1:50,000; the width of Woodward Avenue, the great spine
leading perpendicular from the river, carrying the city grid with it to meet
the Jefferson Ordnance. These boulevards were grand, but not too grand to
walk across, and they became the bone structure for the growth of Detroit.
In the event only the first portion of the Woodward plan was built out, but it
endowed the city with a strong sense of centre, and a strong relationship to
the river which it still has today.

Its centredness is the first paradox in the story of Detroit; the first of
several which will unfold themselves in the following pages. It was the
converging avenues of Detroit, so good for orientation and movement
and so affirmative of the primacy of Downtown, which contributed to its
increasingly unmanageable congestion over the first half of the 20th century
through the rise of the motorcar. The second paradox of Detroit, which has
been much written about, in far more depth and detail than this book can
contain, is that the motorcar itself was both the making and at the same
time the undoing of the city.

Motor City

In 1901 there was another fire in Detroit which proved significant for its
development. Ransom E Olds's car factory was destroyed, including all but

the smallest of his prototypes. The little 'Merry Oldsmobile', which happened to be sitting by the door, was pushed outside to safety by the only person in the building at the time. Through its production, manufacturing techniques moved onto an entirely new scale, with far-reaching social, economic and environmental implications for the five-decade motor boom which was to follow. Olds took the salvaged prototype to the nearby bicycle works of John and Horace Dodge and with them set up an early form of mass production, the precursor of the ground-breaking Oldsmobile assembly line at Lansing which enabled Olds to become America's first auto-millionaire and set the wheels of the growth of the city in motion; 'Come away with me, Lucille / In my merry Oldsmobile'.[5]

Vincent Bryan and Gus Edwards, 'In my Merry Oldsmobile', 1905
Detroit – the location of the love affair with the automobile, commemorated in song.

However, no one had a greater influence on Detroit, and on the rescaling of the city worldwide, than Henry Ford. As well as being the great pioneer of the motorcar, and industrial production methods, Ford was an extraordinary social engineer. While on one hand he led the way in making production lines more and more efficient through the robotic repetition of tasks by men and women, he was on the other hand a great innovator for the wellbeing of his workforce. As the demand for motorcars spread like wildfire across America, competition for labour with Olds, Dodge, Packard, Chrysler and the other manufacturers became a major part of the production equation. Ford's answer, both fiercely competitive and generous at the same time, was the 'five-dollar day'. Five dollars was almost double the going rate for factory labour but, on condition that employees passed an inspection by the Ford Sociological Inspectors at the family home, relating to hygiene, domestic management and family values, they would be entitled to this reward. As well as building and motivating the workforce, there was an ulterior motive in enriching his staff in this way. Ford was selling cars to his

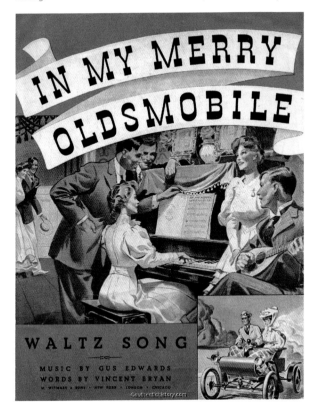

THE "MELTING POT" OF THE ENGLISH SCHOOL OF THE FORD MOTOR COMPANY AT DETROIT

The Ford English School's
graduation ceremony,
Detroit, 1917
Where foreign factory
workers were transformed
into 'standardised
Americans'.

own staff and as a consequence Motor City boomed, not just in production
but also in ownership and use of the automobile.

The question of scale, at the level of society (for which cities are both an
implement and a product), lies at the heart of Fordist philosophy. So great
was Ford's controlling universalism, an equivalent of Jefferson's equalising
grid, that the foreign members of his labour force were required to 'graduate'
into American society, courtesy of Henry Ford. 'These men of many nations
must be taught American ways, the English language and the right way
to live.'[6] The graduation ceremony from the Ford English School involved
workers, who came from all around the world, appearing on stage in their
traditional costumes. They would mount a gangplank on one side of an Ellis
Island packet boat known as the 'melting pot'.[7] Doing a quick change inside,
while six instructors appeared to be stirring the interior with long ladles, they
would appear from the other side dressed in suits and ties; standardised
Americans, 'like standardised parts in the factory where they worked.'[8]

The phrase 'big is beautiful' is often associated with America. This may
indeed relate to physical size; but if, like Ford's attitudes to employment,
it means 'thinking big' in terms of social systems, then for a city like

Detroit there was a danger of over-simplification. If the city is treated like a mechanical system made up of machined parts, rather than a large complex organism, then it will not thrive from generation to generation. The philosophy of the assembly line – its mechanism of growth – was one of Detroit's strengths, but it also became one of its weaknesses and contributed to its shrinkage physically, economically and in terms of outlook.

In 1900, Detroit, which had a wide manufacturing base including trains, bicycles, marine parts, stoves and drugs, had a population of some 900,000. In 20 years it had almost doubled and the spread of car-based suburbia, fuelled by Ford's vision, had begun. Nonetheless, until after World War Two, the city core was very much intact and was well connected to the surrounding neighbourhoods. Meanwhile the streetcar system was second to none, reaching out to the furthest edges of the city. Downtown was the home to more theatres per capita than any other city in the world, and the world's largest American flag flew above the world's tallest department store: Hudson's, overlooking Campus Martius at the heart of the city core. Ironically however, the city of cars failed to integrate its transport systems

Traffic at the intersection of Woodward and Michigan Avenues, Detroit, pre-1930
The Golden Age of Detroit, the city of the car, before the car began to destroy it.

and did not solve the problem of parking. Hudson's had no car park and neither did the impressive Michigan Central Railroad Station of 1913, now abandoned, which was disconnected from the downtown, set remotely in Roosevelt Park on the west of the city.[9] As car use grew, in spite of the creation of Grand Boulevard and the 'New Center' in the 1920s, the city centre became impossibly congested.

Definitions

At this point it is important to define two linguistic distinctions; the words size and scale; the words expansion and growth. As the size of the city increased, how did its scale change? As the city expanded, what was the nature of its growth? The word 'scale', used in the terms of this book, is qualitative. It speaks of relativities as well as values and is just as relevant when viewing a city as a whole, or when touching the detail of a wall or a window frame. The word 'size' is quantitative and can refer either to the size of the population or to its physical extent which, in the case of Detroit, are disproportionately related due to the sprawling nature of the city.

In terms of size, Detroit expanded greatly in the first half of the 20th century – from an area of 10 to 140 square miles (26 to 360 square kilometres),

Warren and Wetmore with Reed and Stem, Michigan Central Railroad Station, Detroit, 1913
An economic phenomenon of bad luck or bad judgement.

reaching a peak population of 1.85 million. Initially however, this was a process of healthy 'growth', like a tree gathering rings over the years, thickening and solidifying, becoming stronger. The city had 'bone structure' – an intense downtown, an inner ring of urban neighbourhoods, an outer ring of factories and beyond that the suburbs; all interwoven by the grid and threaded through by its radiating avenues. It was an integrated anatomical system; the bloodstream, nervous system and major and minor organs all working together. Like a body, it had a well-graded hierarchy of scales.

Whether we take the view of the designer or the dweller of cities, this is a more complex notion than Judge Woodward's simply making sure that Detroit's streets were sized for future expansion. It is a responsive structure of layers and networks; a graded continuum which acknowledges the importance both of compactness in the city plan and of generosity in the city block. It is a structure built up through 'intermediary scale' which can embrace the economic and environmental life cycles of urban components – a neighbourhood or a street, a warehouse or a house, a park or a garden – while taking account of the practical necessity for comfortable movement through the city. It is also a means to achieving a structured backdrop for our lives with which we can connect and which in turn can lift our spirits. This is an example of the first thesis of the book: that 'Intermediary Scale' is a fundamental part of making successful cities, or parts of cities or buildings, or parts of buildings – at all scales. It is a notion which we will revisit in subsequent chapters.

The American Dream

Speaking to Jerry Herron, Dean of American Studies at Wayne State University in Detroit, who has lived in Detroit for over thirty years, stereotypes such as 'Americans like space; their car is an extension of the family' were discussed. Herron suggested that 'for Americans, the city is just a means to an end; their dream is to move out to a house, with a garage and some distance from the neighbors, as soon as they can afford to own a car'.[10] In the words of Alan Cobb, Head of Design at Albert Kahn Associates, the architects of the majority of Detroit's boom-time buildings, 'Detroit was the birthplace of the American dream'.[11]

The negative side of this positive coin for Detroit was that the pattern of car-dependent growth was unsustainable, on the basis of a universalised

The great American Dream
The car is part of the family.

sprawling suburbia which gradually became a challenge to the city's heart and soul. It was a direct working out of Henry Ford's often quoted statement from 1922 that 'The city is doomed [...] We shall solve the city problem by leaving the city.'[12] The desire for space, and a preference for independence over interdependence go back centuries in Detroit; back to the pioneering days. For Detroit, this combined with a commodity-based (car-based) culture of consumption and a liking for social stratification by wealth, and community segregation by race, to create a city lacking in resilience in the event that its good times should turn bad.

After the Boom

Returning to the story of the city, World War Two was good for Detroit. The car plants were turned over to munitions for a period and business boomed. The city peaked in the early 1950s but then became victim of further paradoxes. Forces which had formerly been good for Detroit turned around. The first problem for the post-war city was at the macro-political level. The Government feared that centralised concentrations of industry were targets for nuclear attack from Russia. They positively encouraged industry to relocate; not just on the outer edges of Detroit but away from it altogether. An added paradox here is that the strength of the city's unions, built up in part through the empowering influence of Henry Ford and others, became a problem for the manufacturers and made it advantageous to move elsewhere. Furthermore, increasing unemployment accelerated due to increasing mechanisation. The production line was doing itself out of a job.

An additional problem was the creation of the new interstate freeways, which cut through the city and encircled its core. This nationwide system of highways was another defence against the Cold War threat; speed and ease of movement around the country by road were promoted as being essential for the national good. Communities were informed that the new highways would bring about 'urban renewal', but at a local level the changes proved disastrous. Hastings Street, the main retail spine of the African American community, became the Chrysler Freeway, Interstate 75; and the main street of the Irish community in Corktown became the Lodge Freeway The primary problem of the freeways was not the severance of movement through the city, since the freeways were set into landscaped cuttings and the street grid carried through; rather, it was the loss of civic identity and cohesion. The real problem was that, with the industrial economy already contracting, urban neighbourhoods were robbed of their identifying heart and their optimism. Notwithstanding the extraordinary blossoming of music in Detroit – the birthplace of Motown – through the 1960s, the inner-city communities lost their strength with which to reinvent themselves, or to renew the urban fabric in a shrinking city.

Moving Out

With the freeways came new ideas for shopping which further took life out of the heart of the city. Under the guiding hand of Victor Gruen, a Modern Movement urbanist from Vienna,[13] the first shopping mall in America was created – Northland. One of the key investors in Northland was Hudson's department store, whose business at the heart of the congested city had been struggling for years. Northland was much admired at the time. In its first incarnation it was an external shopping precinct, but with all the convenience of an indoor mall. Easy road access and ample parking, combined with pleasant external spaces, a pioneering art programme and good contemporary design made it into the major magnet for shopping in

Skidmore, Owings & Merrill, the General Motors Building, 1977, seen from the Chrysler Freeway, Interstate 75, Detroit
The freeways cut through the city, leaving deep scars.

Detroit. Today it is just another 'big box' mall among many which collectively fail in their unacknowledged duty to use retail to stitch the city together and contribute to its 'grading of scales'.

'Enclave urbanism' had now taken over. Pockets of relative prosperity were connected by roads and comfortably buffered from each other by driveable distances and greenery. New developments spread further and further out, as residents were happy to buy a new property in a new suburb, with the help of a favourable mortgage market and low petrol prices, instead of restoring an old one closer to the centre. For every new suburban enclave, its inverse appeared within the city: a pocket of empty buildings and vacant, valueless land, like an apple with a rotting core. This condition would be problematic enough in a climate of economic growth but it amounted to a 'vicious circle' of decline in the case of Detroit's shrinking economy. In 1961 Jane Jacobs described the city as being 'largely composed, today, of seemingly endless square miles of low-density failure'.[14]

The impossible conflict which Detroit was falling blindly into was that of still expanding dimensionally while at the same time shrinking in terms of population, industry, employment and economy. The biggest voids appeared with the closing of the large automobile plants which ringed the city centre, but Downtown was also falling apart. In 1981 Jerry Herron arrived in Detroit and, needing ink for his fountain pen, he went to the downtown Hudson's – a pale shadow of its former self – and asked for ink in the pen department. He was met with the reply 'we don't sell ink any more'. In 1986, Hudson's was dynamited, completing the cycle from the awakening of the city

Albert Kahn, the Packard Plant, Detroit, 1903
Nature is taking over.

centre to its being shrouded in a deep sleep. A bike ride from the Northern Engineering Works, through Eastern Market and round to Corktown showed the extraordinary scale of emptiness; a problem on a massive scale, or an opportunity, depending on the viewpoint.

Smith, Hinchman, & Grylls, Hudson's department store, Detroit, 1911, being demolished on 24 October 1998
The destruction of what was once the tallest shop in the world.

Today and Tomorrow

My own visit to Detroit in July of 2013 was memorable. Fallow years can be good for the fields. My first impression, apart from the fact that the downtown core is remarkably well maintained, cordoned off by a little elevated train, was the overwhelming presence of wild nature in the inner urban ring – both the worn-out residential and disused industrial land – immediately surrounding Downtown.

The riverside park in Detroit's Downtown, formerly the city's industrial waterfront
The grassy mound is made of rubble from demolished factories.

Abandoned buildings, Downtown, Detroit: drawing by the author, 2013
Missing teeth characterise the face of the city.

I walked the newly made river edge through long grasses – the place where I was attacked by the bird. It is well put together, but this is a city with many missing teeth: the black voids of empty windows, sometimes showing sky beyond. I have never seen so many windows broken, neither occupied nor even boarded up, taking up the majority of a street frontage; gaping and accidental. Like a grand tourist to Rome in the 18th century, I went to pay homage to the derelict Packard Plant and ponder how are the mighty fallen, and on the way I chose my favourite derelict house – on Grand Boulevard no

less – and imagined setting up home there. The combination of verdant green and deep rust hues, broken glass among ad hoc gardens, mingled with the sound of cocks crowing and a calm feeling in the air, was quite intoxicating.

In Ayn Rand's prophetic words from her 1957 novel *Atlas Shrugged* (based on Detroit): 'A few houses still stood within the skeleton of what had once been an industrial town. Everything that could move, had moved away; but some human beings had remained. The empty structures were vertical rubble; they had been eaten, not by time, but by men [...].'[15] However, according to the Detroit Future City – Strategic Framework Plan, dated December 2012, 'the demolition programme has slowed and is transitioning to reconstruction and rehabilitation'.[16] I read that before the city declared bankruptcy on 18 July 2013.

Grand Avenue, Detroit
One of the thousands of abandoned houses along this once-grand street.

There are apparently some 50,000 empty buildings in central Detroit and, at $5 per square foot (approximately $50 per square metre), this is fertile ground for new businesses. In spite of dire population and unemployment figures, companies headquartered there such as Quicken Loans and Compuware are booming. A new streetcar is being planned for Woodward, Wayne State University has 20,000 students living on campus where 10 years ago it had next to none, and even the car industry is finding new energy in innovation.[17] Young loft-dwellers are moving in, Whole Foods Market has just set up in Midtown and the arts scene is thriving, not just in the field of graffiti.

The facts however are bracing: Detroit, now bankrupt, owes money to more than 100,000 creditors; it is $20 billion in debt. In 1960, the city of Detroit actually had the highest per-capita income in the entire nation, but its manufacturing jobs have shrunk to less than 10 per cent of what they were then and its population has shrunk by over 60 per cent in 60 years.

Dubois Street, Detroit
Dereliction: the boundaries
between public and private
realms are blurred.

About one-third of the city's 140 square miles (360 square kilometres) is
now either vacant or derelict, with 78,000 abandoned homes and houses
for sale for $500 or less. Forty-seven per cent of the population are illiterate
and over half are unemployed.[18] The violent crime rate in Detroit is five
times higher than the national average, and the police solve less than 10 per
cent of the crimes that are committed. But sitting at Slows diner, famous
in the city for bringing new life (and very good food) to the once-buzzing,
now down-at-heel Michigan Avenue, looking across the road at a 'boutique'
hotel and the abandoned railroad station, the rawness of the scene reminds
me of Detroit's rural roots. The edgy signage, the patchwork of bohemian
fringe projects and the out-on-the-porch atmosphere of the place seem to
be fed by a positive nostalgia with very positive possibilities for the future.
It is a collective memory, both of the limitless forests surrounding the city
which were so important for its pre-industrial beginnings, and of its golden
age of industry and innovation.

The Detroit Strategic Framework Plan prophesies the state of the city in 2050 as follows:

> Detroit regains its position as one of the most competitive cities in the nation, the top employment center in the region, and a global leader in technology and innovation, creating a healthy and sustainable jobs-to-residents ratio and economic opportunities for a broad range of residents. Traditional and mixed-use neighborhoods of the city, including city center, district centers and live+make areas, have filled their density capacities and opportunities for new residential growth can be expanded into green residential areas. Productive and ecological landscapes are now firmly established as the new form and image of the city.[19]

It brings us back to the question of 'scale' and 'growth'. If a city grows (as opposed to just expanding), where does it grow from? If it shrinks, what does it shrink back to?

Detroit boomed through the vastness of a new industry, but that is not the only way to grow. Small-scale growth within a big frame of opportunity could in the end be a more robust model. Detroit's first growth was flawed due to its over-reliance on commodities: new houses in new neighbourhoods, served by new shopping malls, highways and cars. Rather, its communities

A park in Corktown, Detroit
A place of contrasts and possibilities.

should have been nurtured as the source of growth. Here again is a form of intermediary scale – that which connects the large to the small, and which connects people to places.

References

1 WG Sebald, *The Rings of Saturn* [*Die Ringe des Saturn*, 1995], Random House (London), 2002, p 159.
2 *Ibid* p 155.
3 The city's motto is 'Speramus Meliora; Resurget Cineribus' – 'We hope for better things; it will rise from the ashes'.
4 L'Enfant in a letter to the President dated 1792, quoted by Spiro Kostof in *The City Shaped: Urban Patterns and Meanings through History*, Thames & Hudson (London), 1991, p 209.
5 *In My Merry Oldsmobile*, words by Vincent Bryan, music by Gus Edwards, 1905:
'Young Johnny Steele has an Oldsmobile, / He loves a dear little girl. / She is the queen of his gas machine, / She has his heart in a whirl. / Now, when they go for a spin, you know, / She tries to learn the auto, so / He lets her steer, while he gets her ear, / And whispers soft and low; /
Come away with me, Lucille / In my merry Oldsmobile, / Down the road of life we'll fly / Automobubbling, you and I. / To the church we'll swiftly steal, / Then our wedding bells will peal, / You can go as far as you like with me, / In my merry Oldsmobile.'
6 Steven Watts, *The People's Tycoon: Henry Ford and the American Century*, Alfred A Knopf (New York), 2005, pp 205–6 and 215.
7 'The Making of New Americans', *Ford Times*, November 1916, p 152: 'Into the gaping pot they went. Then six instructors from the Ford school, with long ladles, started stirring. "Stir! Stir!" urged the superintendent of the school. The six bent to greater efforts. From the pot fluttered a flag, held high, then the first of the finished product of the pot appeared, waving his hat. The crowd cheered [...] many followed [...] on each side of the cauldron. In contrast to the shabby rags they wore when they were unloaded from the ship, all wore neat suits [...] American in looks.' See also Elana Firsht, '"Assembly Line Americanisation:" Henry Ford's Progressive Politics', *Michigan Journal of History*, Fall 2012.
8 Samuel Marquis, head of the Ford Sociological Department, quoted in Stephen Meyer III, *The Five Dollar Day: Labour Management and Social Control in the Ford Motor Company 1908–1921*, State University of New York Press (Albany, NY), 1981, p 157.
9 The unsuccessful location of the station, a product of the optimistic spirit of Daniel Burnham's 'City Beautiful' movement, was another symptom of the latent desire for big spaces which was so formative for Detroit. However, its distance from the city core was ill-judged. 'Make no little plans; they have no magic to stir men's blood [...] Make big plans; aim high in hope and work, remembering that a noble, logical diagram once recorded will never die, but long after we are gone will be a living thing [...] .' Daniel H Burnham speaking at the Town Planning Conference 1910, London.
10 Jerry Herron, Dean of American Studies at Wayne State University, in conversation with the author, July 2013.
11 Alan Cobb, Head of Design at Albert Kahn Associates, in conversation with the author, July 2013.
12 Henry Ford, in a Dearborn-

published article 1922, quoted by Kenneth T Jackson in *Crabgrass Frontier: The Suburbanization of the United States*, Oxford University Press (New York), 1985, p 175: 'The city is doomed [...] the modern city is the most unlovely and artificial sight this planet affords. The ultimate solution is to abandon it. We shall solve the city problem by leaving the city.'

13 See M Jeffrey Hardwick, *Mall Maker: Victor Gruen,* *Architect of an American Dream*, University of Pennsylvania Press (Philadelphia, PA), 2009, which quotes Victor Gruen's words from a talk at the Architectural Association, London in 1970: 'I am often called the father of the shopping mall. I would like to take this opportunity to disclaim paternity once and for all. I refuse to pay alimony to those bastard developments. They destroyed our cities.'

14 Jane Jacobs, *The Death and* *Life of Great American Cities* [1961], Vintage Books (New York), 1992, p 204.

15 Ayn Rand, *Atlas Shrugged*, Random House (New York), 1957, p 159.

16 Detroit Future City – Strategic Framework Plan, dated December 2012, p 30.

17 United States Census Bureau, City-Data.com.

18 Sam Ro, '11 Depressing Facts about Detroit', *Business Insider*, 11 July 2013.

19 Detroit Future City, p 31.

On Scale and Movement

2

'The relation of the city to its parts is similar to that of the human body to its parts; the streets are the veins.'

Francesco di Giorgio Martini, *Trattato di Architettura, Ingegneria e Arte Militare*, 1485[1]

The word 'dimension' has a double meaning; both the simple quantitative measure of a line or a pixel and the more complex aspects of time and space, built up in layers of perception and memory, purpose and understanding. This chapter is about distance and the perception of distance. It is also about choice and freedom; how we choose to move and how this affects our experience of scale in cities. Cities are shaped by, and grow through, their transport systems which, however large a metropolis becomes, if well designed and properly linked together, can help to make an individual feel at home in the city; to feel that the city belongs to them and them to it. The hugeness of a city, when broken down into journeys of twenty minutes here, half an hour there, sometimes by car, by train, by bike or by foot, becomes manageable. As cities grow, they can also shrink in terms of the perception of those who inhabit and use them.

Paris 1925

As we have already seen in connection with Detroit, the car changed

Gradually, Edge becomes Centre

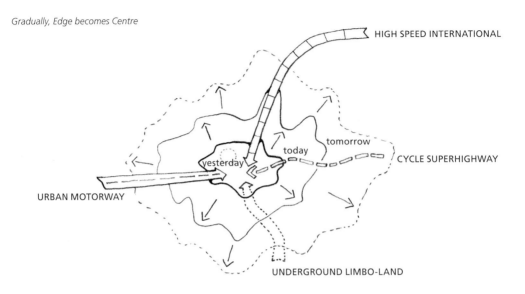

HIGH SPEED INTERNATIONAL

tomorrow

today

yesterday

CYCLE SUPERHIGHWAY

URBAN MOTORWAY

UNDERGROUND LIMBO-LAND

FLYOVER

SUBWAY

Major infrastructure transforms our experience – and the scale – of the city. However, our scale gauge for understanding it is the fine grain weave of buses + trains, taxis + rickshaws, bikes + Segways, footpaths + friendships which binds the city together.

the nature of the city for ever. It is an important part of our lives and an essential piece of the urban equation. It is just as much a source of trouble, however, as it is an asset. As quoted in Willy Boesiger and Hans Girsberger's compendium *Le Corbusier 1910–65*: 'In 1929 the question of Paris stood in a very serious state of uncertainty, since the arrival of the automobile unfolded its consequences and the city became impracticable.'[2]

In 1925, some three years after Henry Ford spoke of the city doomed, Le Corbusier went to see the heads of Peugeot, Citroën and Voisin in Paris and

As the city grows it shrinks: drawing by the author, 2014
Gradually, Edge becomes Centre.

said to them: 'The motor has killed the great city. The motor must save the great city.'[3] Paris had been booming a century ahead of Detroit and on a much larger scale, and its ancient city fabric, centuries older than Detroit's all-new plan, could not cope, particularly as the motorcar began to fill up the streets. Having had no luck with Peugeot and Citroën – 'M. Citroën very amiably replied that he did not know what I was talking about and did not see what the motor-car had to with the problem of the centre of Paris'[4] –

A street in the Marais, Paris
This historic neighbourhood became a slum through the 19th century and, according to Le Corbusier's vision, would have been replaced by an area of skyscrapers and motorways.

Le Corbusier persuaded the Voisin car company to sponsor his speculative project to demolish the Marais district and replace it with an array of new towers linked by motorways. The Marais, on the Right Bank of the Seine, having been home to many of the grandest buildings and spaces of the city in the 16th and 17th centuries, adorned by aristocratic names such as Soubise, de Sully and d'Albret, had fallen into disrepair through the 19th century, due to the migration of the aristocracy to the Left Bank, to the point where by the 1920s it was an infamous slum. Le Corbusier's answer was simple:

> Thenceforward, instead of a flattened-out and jumbled city such as the airplane reveals to us for the first time, terrifying in its confusion, our city rises vertical to the sky, open to light and air, clear, radiant and sparkling. […] Imagine all this junk, which till now has lain spread out over the soil like a dry crust, cleaned off and carted away and replaced by immense clear crystals of glass, rising to a height of 600 feet [180 metres], each at a good distance from the next.[5]

Le Corbusier, A Contemporary City, from *Urbanisme [The City of Tomorrow and its Planning]*, 1924
The Marais redeveloped to accommodate the car, with a mere 5% of the surface area used for buildings, and the remaining 95% devoted to traffic routes, car parks and open spaces.

29711
FONDATION LE CORBUSIER

A new main spine would run from east to west through the city, 130 metres (430 feet) wide without crossroads. Street widths and frequency of crossings would be scaled up by a factor of 10 compared with Old Paris and, while only 5 per cent of the city's land would be used for buildings, the rest being given over to 'speedways, car parks and open spaces',[6] the density of habitation would be quadrupled, on account of the height of the tall buildings.

In his 1924 manifesto entitled *Urbanisme* [translated as *The City of To-morrow and its Planning*], Le Corbusier was reacting to the problems of a fast-changing city and the political and economic trauma of Europe between the wars: out with the old, in with the new. His mistakes as an urbanist, which are as significant as his leaps of genius as an architect, seem obvious now. In Alain de Botton's words, 'The plan seemed so obviously demented that it intrigued me.'[7] Surprisingly however, they are still very relevant to the makers of cities today. Le Corbusier's errors of scale in the Plan Voisin, apart from proposing the destruction of one of the most important historic neighbourhoods in Paris (which fortunately, preserved from his scheme and since restored to its former glory, is today one of the city's most prestigious and highly valued ancient quarters), are twofold: firstly that this was a car-focused vision, with little acknowledgement of other means of transport; and secondly that he simply misjudged distances and the proportions of spaces needed to create a comfortable urban environment. It is natural for people to prefer closeness to distance, within reason. Apart from the obvious practical benefits, it appeals to the child in us all; we like cosiness in a house, we like cosiness in a city. Just as in a house we can move from the more public rooms to more intimate spaces, from the living room to the garden or from the hallway to the porch, in a way which is connected with the fabric of the house (we can touch the house), so too in a city, albeit on a larger scale, there is a range of movements by a variety of means – foot, bicycle, tram, train, car – which enable us to connect with our environment as a smoothly graded continuum rather than a fragmentary set of experiences. It is odd that Le Corbusier, the creator of one the century's most important theories of human scale, the Modulor – an all-encompassing and highly sensitised system of scale based on the broadly normative size and proportion of all human beings[8] – should not have applied a similar insight to urban design.

As an 'urban machine', Le Corbusier's Ville Radieuse would never have become the smooth-running utopia he had in mind. More deeply than that, however, he failed to acknowledge the organic nature of the city, rather insisting on a mechanistic model. The body analogy, quoted at the start of the chapter from Francesco di Giorgio Martini, the 15th-century Sienese painter and architect, is strong.[9] The city is fed by flows; populations in motion are the blood. The circulatory system connects up the major and minor organs, the spaces and places of the city, and contains many elements – white cells, red cells, plasma; modes of transport, activity, people – which together make up the workings of a healthy body. The interconnectedness of transport systems, and of squares and streets and highways, rivers, railways and bike paths, is essential to achieving the intermediary scale – the human scale-ratio – which can make the difference between a good piece of city and a bad one.

Like a human body also, the city is made up of many interconnected chambers of varying size and function. A journey from a front garden to a railway station by bicycle, along a street, under a motorway, across a park, down a lane between houses; a train journey into the city and a walk over a river, across a grand square, along a busy shopping street, through a narrow arched passageway and into a small urban courtyard surrounded by buildings; up steps, to linger in a porch and wait for the door to be opened; this can be part of the healthy pattern of our physical experience. It is the graded nature of our spatial experience – private and public, indoor and outdoor, static and dynamic – which connects us to our physical environment. This is the measure with which cities are appreciated and, hopefully, designed. Without a range of well-connected scales and modes of transport available to us, it will be hard to feel 'at home' in the city, but this goes beyond physical movement and sensation. We function continually at scales beyond our own by means of memory and the imagination.

Absolutes and Relativities

To build on the first thesis of this book (Chapter 1) – that intermediary scale is an essential part of making successful cities and enabling a comfortable and coherent understanding of the urban realm, at all scales – the second thesis is that there are certain normative absolutes of scale in the making of cities, including both the mechanics and psychology of movement, which relate back to the human body, binding all people together consciously or unconsciously, and should therefore guide urban designers in their work.

Fifty metres (165 feet) is a short distance to walk before being able to turn left or right; 100 metres (330 feet) is quite long; and arguably 200 metres

(660 feet) is too long. The city is porous; it is permeated by the movement of people. Degrees of porosity in the city influence deeply the habits and feelings of its inhabitants. In terms of width, 15 to 20 metres (50 to 65 feet) is reasonable for a street (although streets much narrower than this are also an essential part of making a good city) and, while 30 metres (100 feet) is wide, 60 metres (200 feet) begins to become too wide to cross with ease. Mechanical constraints such as volume and speed of traffic and layout of utilities will dictate street width; but, in an ideal city, human comfort needs to be the highest priority. Narrower streets are easier to cross, however in northern climates, deep dark canyons can be oppressive. From inside buildings, everyone likes good daylight and no one likes to be too close to the windows opposite. A balance has to be struck. 'Rules of thumb' such as these, which are well studied in the Danish urbanist Jan Gehl's book *Cities for People*,[10] can be treated as rough but universal checks for the scaling of a city, even though perceptions of distance vary in relation to both the mode of travel and the context of person, time and place.

The interrelation of the quantitative and qualitative aspects of movement are at the same time cultural and experiential. Distance and the perception of distance fluctuate according to speed and how we feel as we travel. We measure journeys quantitatively, more in terms of time than in distance – 'it's only twenty minutes away'. Traditionally neighbourhoods have often developed around focal points, such as churches and mosques, to be within easy walking distance. The word 'easy' means different things in hot or cooler climates. Dust, noise and access to shade are all factors in judging distance. Steve Mouzon in his study of movement, 'Walk Appeal', challenges the accepted 'quarter-mile' measure – 5 minutes by foot – as being a factor of quality, not quantity. He compares a 'power centre' in Middle America with the Campus Martius in Rome. At the former, people will drive even the shortest distances, 'not because they're lazy, but because it's such a terrible walking experience';[11] meanwhile it is normal for us all to equate complex vectors of time and distance, and assess factors of possible delay, simply in order to decide how to move from A to B. Conversely there are terrible driving experiences, for example getting stuck in a traffic jam or finding it impossible to park, which lead to people choosing to leave their car at home.

In spite of the fact that this book is all about relativities, and the very notion of scale, both physical and perceived, is relative, it is nonetheless important to acknowledge that there can be such a thing as a 'right' or 'wrong' scale for each of us; it gives us a measure with which to gauge success. The width of a street and the ease with which we can cross it is an example. Park Avenue in New York can feel daunting to cross at only 40 metres (130 feet), and the Champs Élysées in Paris at 70 metres (230 feet) has gone beyond a normative comfortable measure for a person on the street to inhabit both sides with ease; to cross it is an undertaking. Meanwhile King Khalid bin Abdul Aziz Street and many others in Abu Dhabi, at 100 metres (330 feet), is too much, even in the cooler months.

For simplicity, our scale-gauge for the city could be said to be calibrated at four scales: the car, public transport, the bicycle and walking. Each of these is relative to environmental quality, to climate, to cultural expectations and to the likelihood of delay. While all modes of movement are integral to our experience and perception of the city, it is consistent with the structure and direction of this book, which zooms from macro to micro, that walking, and the raw experience of the city when on foot, should provide the base measure with which to judge sizes and distances of streets, blocks and neighbourhoods, and the nature of connections between them.

The Car: A Deceptive Measure

The car and a car-based city are contradictory in many ways. In one sense a good road system makes places feel closer, but in another sense, in the words of Christopher Alexander, 'cars turn towns to mincemeat',[12] and distances can seem further than they are, not simply as a factor of time, but also of character. The story of highways scarring the city, from which Paris

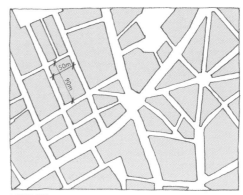

LONDON

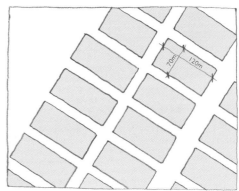

NEW YORK

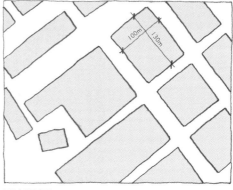

ABU DHABI

The dimensions of three cities compared: drawings by the author, 2014
As we move through the city, the sizing of urban blocks becomes our measure of its scale.

escaped relatively lightly, is found the world over, from Detroit to Doha to London. It is easy to enjoy, with some guilt, the feeling of closeness to central London which the Great West Road gives to the western suburbs of Hammersmith and Chiswick – only 20 minutes' drive with no traffic. It is hard to be entirely negative about this urban motorway, even though it cuts through neighbourhoods in a callous and damaging way. The cinematic experience of slicing through west London in a car, traffic permitting, is not only convenient but can be a pleasure, but it is very much at the expense of the local journey by bike or foot, from the high road to the river where formerly pleasant terraces have been amputated by the motorway and quiet streets reconnected by dank underpasses. Even with eyes closed, crossing it is a harsh experience – the noise and the fume-filled air numb the senses – but we are a resilient race and these areas have survived nonetheless as good places to live.

This and the Great West Road were part of the plan for making London into a 'motorway box' which originated in Patrick Abercrombie and John Henry Forshaw's County of London Plan of 1943 – a plight which was averted in the 1970s thanks to initiatives such as the campaign to save Covent Garden in London's West End which at the time was threatened with demolition to

Great West Road, London
This harsh urban motorway has sliced through a charming neighbourhood, near the River Thames. Nonetheless the area has not lost its character, and the road-users rejoice in how easily it gets them to the centre of town.

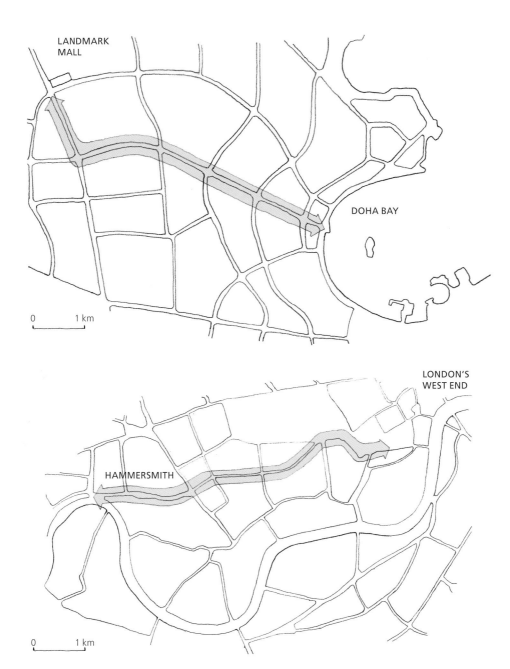

LANDMARK
MALL

DOHA BAY

0   1 km

LONDON'S
WEST END

HAMMERSMITH

0   1 km

From Hammersmith to the West End of London and from West Bay to Landmark Mall in Doha: drawings by the author at the same scale, 2014
If we compare the map of these two journeys, it is hard to correlate the two. The undeveloped expanses and huge highways in Doha make a short journey feel longer.

make way for a conference centre and a new road system. To quote SPC Plowden of the Covent Garden Community Association, 'roads go in lines, character does not'.[13] Cities such as Birmingham or Coventry were not so lucky and found their centres severed from their suburbs. These are wounds which take a long time to heal.

If we compare the journey along the Great West Road with one of similar distance in a car-based city, such as the drive from West Bay to Landmark Mall in Doha, Qatar, the latter feels much further, even though with no traffic it can be far quicker. The fact that one drives on large roads at high speeds through open tracts of unfinished city, with no sense of orientation or connection – with scant chance of building a mental map – perceptually makes distances seem greater than they are. The car becomes a barrier and exaggerates the effect of separation between the people in the vehicle and the places they are passing through; between one piece of the city and the next. This is what produces the 'enclave city'.

West Bay – Doha's Central Business District, which covers an area the same size as Soho, Mayfair and Fitzrovia in London – is a phenomenon. It is entirely designed for the car and is almost impossible to walk, both because of the inadequacy of the footpaths and crossings, and also due to the lack of shade. But ironically it is no easier to navigate by car. A journey can take two or three times as long as it should, simply because of one-way systems, roundabouts and a counterintuitive road system. It is a common experience to be able to see one's destination, one of the awkward looking-glass-and-metal towers some distance away, but find it almost impossible to get there, either by car or by foot. The fact that West Bay has been created within the last 20 years, through a period of relative enlightenment in the field of urban design, is evidence that observations which may seem obvious in this text are still worth making, and are particularly relevant to new areas of cities being laid out at high speed around the world (fast urbanism), where the car is the primary end user, rather than the pedestrian.

The perception of distances, and how cities hold together, from the perspective of the motorcar, are also affected by traffic flows and traffic jams – like the workings of a healthy bloodstream – and the price of fuel, congestion charging, and parking costs and availability. There is a self-regulating balance to be achieved, but not without central investment in infrastructure. In terms of transport, choice – and the stitching together of

TORNADO

20th Aug 2011

all modes to make a seamless fabric – is the key to making a city which can feel like home.

West Bay, Doha: drawing by the author, 2009
A melange of towers and traffic.

The Train: Recalibrating the City

However well-designed a city's road system might be, it has a limited future without mass public transport. The 'Law of Impatience' governs most of our choices of how to move about in cities. We are generally seeking the quickest, and preferably the cheapest, way to travel from A to B. Reliability, frequency of service, comfort and quality of information are also factors in how we choose to move around and in how we perceive time and distance.

The new metro in Dubai was predicted to be a waste of money since Emiratis were so attached to the comfort and privacy of their cars that it was thought they would never use it. Although it is still a rudimentary system, serving only some of the major nodes in the city, and air-conditioned walkways are in some cases exceedingly long in order to bridge

A Segway troop in Washington
Intermediary modes of transport such as Segways and bicycle rickshaws enable people to transcend the limitations of walking, while maintaining direct contact with the sounds, smells and sensations of the city.

over 12-lane motorways and make connections between areas which were only designed for the car, nonetheless the new metro is well used and is already prompting the increase of densities around the stations. Robert Wright, writing in the *Financial Times*, describes the Dubai metro as 'sometimes uncomfortably full' but he still considers that it is 'playing an important role in knitting Dubai together'.[14] He states that although only 7 per cent of the passengers are Emirati, this is more than was expected. Special carriages are provided for the 'Gold Class' and for women and children. To complete the knitted fabric of a local public transport system, the role of buses, trams, taxis, rickshaws and even Segways must not be forgotten about. The grading of transport modes from long journeys to short, from the scale of the city to the scale of the neighbourhood, is a fundamental part of successful city making.

Railways and metros are directly connected to growth, in terms of both expanse and density. The ambitious 'Grand Paris' project leads the way in rail-based urbanism. 'Paris must become bigger than Paris. We must give the metropolitan area the means to act at the right scale. It is a national issue,' said President François Hollande to members of Parliament and of the Paris City Council in January 2013.[15] The project involves 200 kilometres (125 miles) of new automated public transport network encircling the capital,

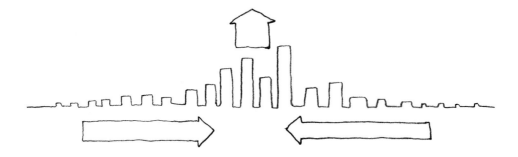

with 72 new or improved stations, catering for 2 to 3 million journeys each day and train waiting times during peak periods reduced to 90 seconds. It will increase the population of the Île de France by a million and will create 1.5 million jobs. In a 2009 *New York Times* article, Nicolai Ouroussoff recalls a meeting with Jean Nouvel, one of the architects involved in Grand Paris, in which Nouvel traced the outer edges of greater Paris on a map, outlining a border roughly 1,000 kilometres (625 miles) long that encircled 'a range of generic middle-class communities', and beyond which was 'rural France, a patchwork of fields and forests'. He continues: 'Nouvel's plan is to create a harder, more defined edge – "a thick band of gardens and fields that come right up to the front door, like a gigantic communal farmers' market. It is a place where you can grow tomatoes, care for children, play sports – a whole ecological life can happen."'[16]

A railway or metro system in a city enables greater density simply by reducing the amount of space needed for cars, car parks and urban motorways. It increases intensity by carrying people in numbers which would be impractical by car. In addition, the city becomes more compact and thus easier to move around by foot and bicycle. It is consolidated. In this way the railway is a recalibration of the city – resetting the measure of the city fabric; like a cloth woven with a finer warp and weft as opposed to a coarse knitted blanket. By giving people the choice not to use their cars, it enables them to become more connected. We are back to 'intermediary scale' again – connecting people and places; enabling people to 'touch' the city in their daily lives. It is paradoxical but somehow not surprising that as a city grows through its railways system, it shrinks. What seemed impossibly faraway destinations are suddenly nearby.

Density, intensity and heights increase towards the centre, while distances diminish: drawing by the author, 2014
Public transport systems enable higher densities, without generating additional traffic or space required for wide roads and car parks.

The focus here has been local transport: joining the city together, adding intensity and giving people more choice of where to live and how to move around, meanwhile enabling it to grow in a healthy way. However, regional and international train services are an essential part of recalibrating our experience of the city. Since I was at university, when to get to Cambridge one had to change at Royston with cold, misty evenings being spent waiting on railway platforms and a journey time of up to two hours, the booming city of academia is now just 45 minutes away from King's Cross and feels like an outrigger of Bloomsbury. With Paris only 165 minutes away, without the complexity of airports and aeroplanes, the world has shrunk. Meanwhile our experience of the city is surely expanded.

Railways can be barriers, particularly when they run at ground level. Traditionally they have brought an element of 'railway blight', a negative aura,

Scale-change by railway: drawing by the author, 2014
New and improved rail connections from King's Cross St Pancras in London to Cambridge and to Paris have brought these places closer to each other.

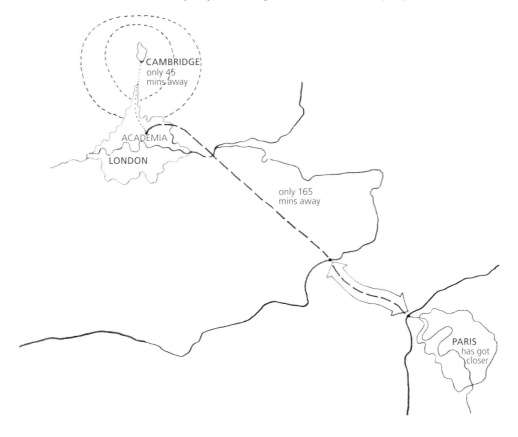

on the land around. But increasingly, stations seem to become positive points within the city's physiognomy, bright hotspots of perceived value. Railways change perceptions. The 'L' rapid transit system in Chicago, a city where in the last 10 years the residential population of the downtown area has grown by 40 per cent,[17] has formed the identity of Downtown and is part of its muscular but habitable scale. Elevated trains such as this and the Docklands Light Railway (DLR) in London become part of the city's intermediary scale in terms of its physical layering as well as its dynamics. Underground systems create a very different experience: a connected limbo-land where movement becomes an abstraction which both connects and disconnects, so much so that when walking from street to train below ground, sometimes taking long and labyrinthine journeys, we lose all sense of time and distance.

The Chicago 'L' at South State Street
Chicago's elevated railway has not only enabled high-density development and easy movement around the city; it also adds a layer of enclosure – an intermediary scale – within the realm of local traffic and pedestrian movement.

Bikes and Neighbourhoods

Buses and, for some cities, trams, add another layer to the scale by which we can understand and move through the city; but the experience of movement is a function of the body, and to feel fully at home in the city – like moving from one room of our house to another, or going next door to visit our parents – requires some direct contact with the sounds, smells and sensations of the street. Cities are too big to walk everywhere. Perhaps in Detroit or Doha, the car works as an extension of the body. In Venice (a city for which it would require a whole other book to discuss movement, urban space and scale), it is the boat that carries this function. When I first visited Amsterdam, where there are more bicycles than residents in the city centre and where more than half of the entire population use a bike every day, I was deeply struck by how bicycles seem to provide the measure for the city – in space, time and motion – by literally being an extension of people's family lives and their physical being. Unlike Britain where cyclists like to dress up in elaborate gear, there is no fuss with a bike in Holland; jump on, jump off, load up the children, go where you like. It seems natural and connected, all aided by dedicated bike paths everywhere. This only works in a city which is relatively flat, but it illustrates how people benefit from having a 'unit of measure' which can relate both to the scale of the city and to the scale of their

A rainy day on Coolsingel, Rotterdam
In Holland, the bicycle is an extension of the body.

bodies. One only has to see how cities including Paris, London and New York have been palpably transformed by the introduction of public rent-a-bike schemes to understand the scaling effect of the bicycle. It fills the gap between public transport and walking; it makes a journey from a 40-minute ordeal into a 15-minute pleasure; it is cheap, reliable, healthy, carbon neutral, fun, and often faster than a car – if only it were safer. Most of all, it gives absolute independence – pure freedom; a rare luxury in an urban world.

My own decision to bicycle to Canary Wharf from Chiswick one sunny day in 2012 – a journey of just over 12 miles (some 20 kilometres) – was a revelation in terms of understanding and rescaling the city. The one-hour ride to the Tower of London was familiar, but beyond that I had no idea of how to get to Canary Wharf except by Underground or taxi; it felt very far away. By taxi the journey felt disconnected by highways and junctions; by Underground it felt like a distant outrigger of the city, albeit easy to get to. Happily, on my bike journey, when I reached Tower Bridge, I found 'Cycle Superhighway Number 3'. The easy ride, through neighbourhoods which only a decade before would have felt threatening, took slightly longer than the light railway which ran above me on its lightweight elevated deck, but it gave me a measure of the city which I had not had before and made me feel a sense of belonging in a place where I had previously felt an alien. The city shrank as I moved east and my own experience – my own touch – was enlarged and enriched.

My search for the ideal cup of coffee in Doha by bike, in the middle of the morning, was not such a success. A five-minute taxi ride should have equated to a 30-minute walk or less than 10 minutes by bike, if only it had been possible. However, what looked close on Google Earth

Cycle Superhighway Number 3, London
It begins at the Tower of London, making the journey to Canary Wharf, which before appeared impossible (except by Underground), seem easy and even enjoyable.

Citi Bike, New York
Public bike rental schemes in
New York, Paris and London
have changed how streets
feel. Casual cyclists feel
they belong in the city, and
the city belongs to them.
A certain scale-connection
is made which does not
exist by foot, car or public
transport.

proved to become a bizarre odyssey of almost an hour by bike, simply
because of the impassable motorways and roundabouts which offered
nothing but grave risk to life and limb to the pedestrian or the pioneering
bicyclist. After that, having ordered a car once or twice, just to get coffee, I
generally went without.

We are talking here all about scale: scale as the perception of size. Time
is absolute but the perception of time expands and contracts, concertina-
fashion, depending on how long we have to wait at a traffic light in a
car, the comfort of a train carriage or the feeling of safety or danger on a
bike path through a park. If we have all the modes of transport discussed
above available to us, all knitted together, then we have a graded, and
interconnected, set of scale-choices with which to make the most of where
we are, as well as being able to move from place to place with the best
balance of speed, comfort and economy.

**Harry Beck, map of the
London Underground,
1933**
A circuit board for London.

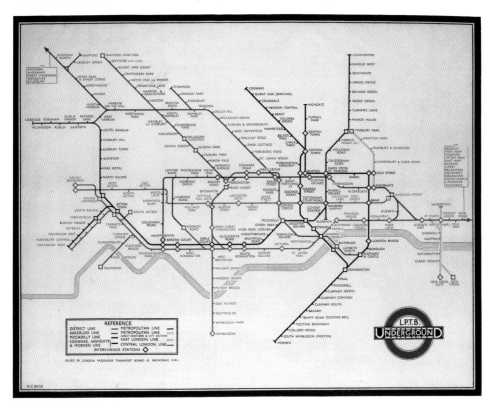

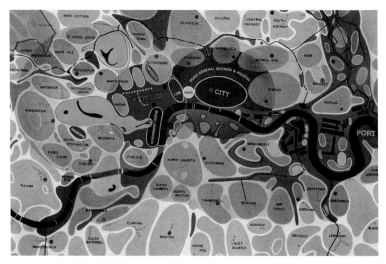

Patrick Abercrombie and
John Forshaw, from the
County of London Plan,
1943
The overlapping villages of
London.

This is good for individuals, but it is good for community too – the making
of the 'home', at the scale of the city. There are two famous maps of
London as a community: Harry Beck's schematic Underground map, first
proposed by him in 1931, and Abercrombie and Forshaw's map of the
villages of London from the County of London Plan. The Underground map
has been much studied and has become an iconic image for London. It
is a circuit-board diagram, showing lines of flow connected by nodes. Its
abstraction – the approximation to the city's actual shape – correlates to the
near-placelessness of the experience of travelling below ground. Mentally
however, and as a practical tool for navigation, it speaks of the connecting up
of neighbourhoods – Camden Town, Royal Oak, Sloane Square, Monument.
The second map, which was described by its creators as 'an idea, a plan
for something that is living, something that is growing',[18] is about 'scaling
the city' for people; it shows how London, perhaps more than any other, is
a city of villages. The city has grown to absorb the villages of Kensington,
Hampstead, Pimlico and Mile End, but they have retained their names and
identities. They overlap, and movement between them is not solely reliant on
either the car or the train.

This is the intermediary scale, or scale-structure, which binds the city
together. Each village is part of a molecular fabric, overlapping and fusing
with its neighbour to make a robust and healthy cellular structure of
interdependent parts.

Walkable City – Msheireb, Doha

'Above all, do not lose your desire to walk. Every day I walk myself into a state of well-being and walk away from illness. I have walked myself into my best thoughts and I know of no thought so burdensome that one cannot walk away from it.'

Søren Aabye Kierkegaard, 1847[19]

The World Jigsaw Company map of London, designed by the author, 2013
Divided by borough and delineated by postcode. Each individual piece of the city can be held in the hand, dismantled and put back together again.

The project in Doha which I have been involved with for many years – Msheireb,[20] in the centre of the old city – is a good example of the value of

making a city walkable, even though it will never be by walking alone that we can fully understand urban scale. It is a large mixed-use development, masterplanned by Arup and AECOM, with Allies and Morrison for whom I was partner in charge, and developed by Msheireb Properties, the property arm of Qatar Foundation. The plan actively promotes walking, in a city where it is almost impossible to go by foot except in the old souk, in shopping malls, along the Corniche or in the few parks. Msheireb (the name means 'place of sweet water') was favoured because of its good water supply and became the first area of the city to be developed after oil revenues began to feed its growth in the late 1940s and early 1950s.

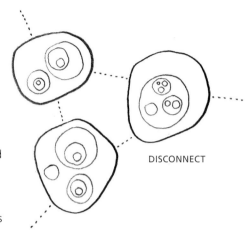

Enclave city: drawing by the author, 2014
Gaps between neighbourhoods, disconnected except by road or rail, prevent the city from fulfilling its potential as the body of a living community.

DISCONNECT

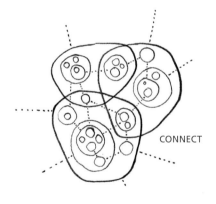

Compact city: drawing by the author, 2014
Overlaps between 'urban villages' enable the 'cell structure' of the city to come alive. Multivalent relationships between the basic units of house, street, block, neighbourhood and district hold the city together, giving it health and strength.

CONNECT

Msheireb is now the subject of a 'fine grain' masterplan; a reworking of old city patterns, as far as possible on the scale of the old city. The blocks are relatively small; generally between 50 and 80 metres (160 to 260 feet) across, and sometimes as little as 25 metres (80 feet). Like a coral reef, the block structure of Msheireb is porous. It is natural when walking through the city to want to zigzag; to follow intuitive lines of desire. Two long straights on main streets will generally not be chosen over multiple short left and right turns through back streets, for those who know their way, if the choice is offered. This masterplan follows the advice of Jane Jacobs in her definitive work, *The Death and Life of Great American Cities*: 'blocks must be short; that is, streets

Msheireb, 'place of sweet water', Doha
A view from the south, with the Amiri Diwan, the Corniche and towers of West Bay beyond, and Souk Waqif to the right. It will become the walkable heart of the city, with plentiful arcades, crossings and traffic-calmed streets.

and opportunities to turn corners must be frequent'.[21] It has been cut up into fine pieces and interlinked with a fine weave, offering many choices for how to move – whether walking the children to school, crossing town from meeting to meeting, exploring the city for the first time or going for a cup of coffee. The distribution of mosques is part of the weave, following traditional guidance; no one should be more than five minutes' walk away from a mosque. This aspect of scaling the city runs deeper than practicality: to find the village in the city, to create walkable units, each with their focal points where people come together, is essential to the static as well as the dynamic aspects of good city-making.

There are several other ways that this piece of the city is being rescaled for the pedestrian. Firstly by the fact that the traffic is calmed; the masterplan has a vast collective infrastructure below ground which allows vehicle movements at street level to be minimised, making the streets easy to cross. Secondly, almost all the walking routes through Msheireb are in the shade, being

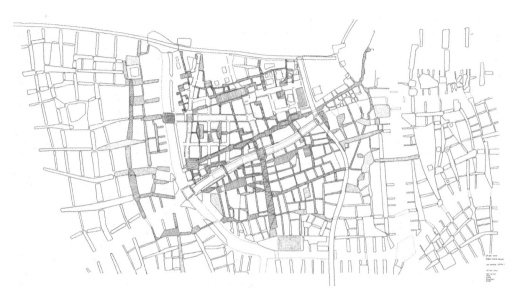

arcaded or sufficiently narrow. It is impossibly hot in the Gulf for two to three months of the year, but for another six months it is pleasant except for the fact that the sun burns; so shade is essential. The simple difference between walking in the shade or in the sun can fundamentally affect our perception of distance; the city can shrink, and our own ability to participate in it can be expanded, if we can walk in comfort.

Thirdly, Msheireb is powerfully connected into the surrounding city fabric by the joining up of streets and walking routes, many of which follow historical lines. An evening stroll westwards along the souk, which is now abruptly cut off by Jassim bin Mohammed Street, will lead to the carved 'souk connection' – an unbroken route following the line of the ancient wadi, the natural channel for flash floods in the rainy season, from which the whole of Msheireb's 35-hectare (86-acre) plan opens up. The lines of Al Rayyan Road and Masat Street are like lines of stitching; connecting the northern edge and the main square of the project with the burial ground (now the city's most central car park). Doha's first illuminated shopping street – Kharaba or Electricity Street – meanders down towards the junction with Salwa Road, the road to Saudi Arabia. This will be the link to Doha's busiest metro station, the crossing of three lines. Abdullah bin Thani Street runs down from the main square to 'jump the gap', to connect seamlessly into Abdul Azeez bin Ahmed Street, the future spine of heritage regeneration in Old Doha. This

Makower Architects, Stitching the City, Doha, 2012
This strategic image shows the streets and spaces of Old Doha as positive volumes. It sets Msheireb at the centre of a public-realm network – connected and navigable by foot, bicycle or rickshaw.

Allies and Morrison, Phase 1B housing, Msheireb, Doha, 2014
All major routes within Msheireb are shaded, either by the narrowness of the streets or by arcades.

and multiple small *sikkat* – narrow lanes, weaving through the masterplan – carry the north–south grain of Doha (the line of the prevailing breeze) across the busy Msheireb Street to humanise what is currently a harsh and worn-out part of the city.

Finally, it is the fine-tuning of the street edge at ground level and the creation of shaded colonnades and cohesive and plenteous crossings which are friends of the pedestrian at Msheireb. Even paving details, giving the pedestrian priority over the car, have been used to promote walking in a city where it is almost unheard of and impossible to do so. A surface of stone paving, to match the pavement, even on a regular carriageway, can make us feel at home in the street in a way which we do not with tarmac. The difference between a high or low kerb can entirely alter how we feel about crossing the road, particularly the ease with which we will choose to jaywalk. Indeed the joy of jaywalking is a measure of a city's homeliness; again it gives intermediary scale, enabling us to connect.

The overriding motto for Msheireb has been to create a piece of city which is rooted in the past while looking to the future, and movement is one important aspect of achieving this. To make a place where walking is easy, in fact positively enjoyable; where one has the choice not to use the car; where one can sit in a quiet square or chain up a bike, or find oneself meandering through narrow lanes, able to imagine 'this is what it must have been like in the past, when life was calmer', without resorting to a false reproduction of the past, but unapologetic in the beauty of nostalgia, is a fine thing: it meets a human need which many would deny. To stitch the city together in time and motion in this way is like producing a well-made woven fabric. For everything to connect, with a diverse array of threads, without loose ends, tears or frays; to create an environment where movement by all manner of means is natural, easy and free, is a fair ideal to pursue.

Air and Ether

It is impossible to finish a chapter on scale and movement without mentioning two important modes of travel – flight and the Internet – both of which raise the question of people and places in different ways, for the future as well as for the present. Both air travel and our experience in cyberspace represent advances in technology, steps forward. They both to some extent involve the loss of contact with our immediate environment, a feeling of placelessness; but paradoxically they are working in opposite directions – the physical and non-physical.

Today 96 per cent of the world's population have a mobile phone, that is 6.8 billion people.[22] Only two and a half billion people use the Internet at the moment, but these figures are increasing at a steepening gradient each year, particularly in developing countries.[23] Only 20 years ago it was almost unknown. Sooner or later the rate of growth will begin to slow, but not yet. Meanwhile the meaning of the word 'address' has changed. The *Oxford English Dictionary* still defines it as 'the place where a person lives or an organization is situated'[24] but its meaning is shifting towards the person rather than the place, wherever they are in the world.

The rise of cyber communications is manifested nowhere more than in the changing nature of retail. Shopping is part and parcel of moving through and interacting with cities, but the Internet is driving a rapid process of evolution. It is extraordinary that in the last decade we have become accustomed to shopping all around the world, and having things delivered to our door, in ways which go far beyond our own capacity for movement. We press a button, blink, and some days later a courier arrives at our door, flesh and blood with a package. We do not think about where he has come from or what journeys the package has made. If we do stop and think about it, it feels more like the huge footsteps of a light-footed giant than an arduous journey by land, air or sea; it seems as easy as spinning the globe on Google Earth. We sign for the parcel, but cannot remember what it cost, and no money has passed from hand to hand; it is surprisingly unsurprising.

The invention of 'Cyber Monday' has been a success. This is the name promoted by world retailers for the Monday in November after US Thanksgiving Day, considered to be the jamboree kick-off for the Christmas shopping season. A billion dollars changed hands in the ether on that day in 2010 and three years later, $1.75 billion.[25] Meanwhile, in the last decade Amazon's yearly sales have increased fourteen-fold,[26] and Blockbuster and Borders, among many retailers large and small, have gone out of business, leading to the closure of thousands of physical shops. Where does the rise of cyber shopping leave the person in the street? The world has shrunk but, unlike the other shrinkages mentioned so far, it seems that our experience is thinned by this rather than being enriched. The world we are dealing with seems to have been flattened, and the sensation of what we are doing is diluted in an environment of easy, instant access.

The survivors of this seismic shift are having to adapt. Local high streets are suffering and larger retailers, while fighting for survival in and out of the shopping malls, their natural habitats, are adding to the plight of the smaller shops which find it less and less easy to compete, making for increasingly generic shopping environments. Nonetheless it feels as if shopping in the flesh is growing in new ways: almost taking the place of religion in some societies, becoming increasingly less utilitarian and more ceremonial. Fast-changing – 'what's new?' – pop-up culture, fed by instant universal access to digital information (and when needed, the ability to spend), is all part of what seems to be a spiralling frenzy of consumption. In some ways this is the healthy pulse of a successful city. Before the Internet, the city or town was the provider of the majority of our needs. Now we are world citizens and the city is less important in that respect, but the role of 'real' shops, markets, restaurants and cafés, as a cultural and social activity if nothing else, will surely never die.

In spite of the fact that using our own home as a place to shop is a very new experience, and our need for public space and physical interaction is to some extent diminishing, a greater distinction is emerging between need and desire. We touch products before we buy them because we want to. We go out on the street among the crowds because it is a good way to keep our children occupied, and we enjoy the buzz: touching the city. With the rise of the Internet and portable communications, as a race, we are at the very early stages of an evolutionary shift, which is fundamentally affecting our sense of place, and thus scale, within the city. It is too early to know whether it will bring about the disintegration of cities, to a greater or lesser degree, or of our familiar relations with them; probably not.

People do like to be together, face to face, whether they live only a few minutes away and meet at the local pub, or many hours away by plane and meet only occasionally. The fact that Skype calls are free, and face to face via camera and screen, ought to mean that fewer people travel by air – choosing speed, ease and economy over the trials and cost of flying, at least some of the time. However, statistics are not yet showing this to be the case. By June 2012, less than a decade after Skype was launched, the number of downloads of Skype to Android devices had passed the 70 million mark;[27] that is the same number of people who pass through Heathrow airport in a year – a facility which is now working at 99 per cent capacity.[28] Globally air travel is indeed on the increase – albeit at a rate of only 3 to 4 per cent – and in only one continent, North America, is it reducing.[29] The overall rise is part of a rebalancing process; a shifting centre of gravity, and increasing prosperity, freedom and industrialisation, towards the East and South of the globe, but the American statistic may be the beginning of a natural decline. Unless a renewable fuel can be found for aeroplanes, the cost of flying gradually ought to rise due to the increasing scarcity of fossil fuels, and this ought to create an economic cap on air travel; but this will take time. In the shorter term however, as with shopping, people may be flying increasingly through desire, and less through need.

Not according to John D Kasarda of the University of North Carolina, whose much-quoted phrase 'the fastest, best-connected places will win'[30] is indicative of a new kind of global competition, perhaps not so much driven by the desire to meet or generate an increasing demand for air travel, as to catch the existing flights by becoming the favoured 'hub' among competing airports. Kasarda describes Dubai as 'the world's first aerotropolis nation – an airline and an airport with a city attached to it'.[31] He rightly builds on the time-honoured truth that it is unnatural for a city to remain stable; it must grow in order not to shrink. He has become known for his far from appealing idea of an 'aerotropolis': a new kind of city with an airport at the centre, of dimensions and connections bigger and better than any other in the vicinity, largely indoors so that the noise of the aeroplanes is not a problem.

Kasarda is right to correlate airport expansion with economic growth. Flight is part of our lives; it is a pump for cities. Doha's new airport, due to open this year, will increase its passenger numbers from 20 million to 50 million; Dubai's from 60 million to 90 million; and Heathrow's capacity would increase from 70 million to a hundred million, if a third runway were built. If the airports do not grow, supply will not be able to feed demand. In terms of a sense of scale, the international mix of a city and its importance as a global transport hub certainly contribute to its economic pulse, and its identity; they help it 'feel big'. For the physical and spatial experience of those who live and work there, however, it remains at the periphery. It is in the very nature of flying, even boarding the train on the way to the airport, to disconnect; only to reconnect when stepping out of the taxi at the other end. In terms of air travel, closeness ceases to matter; it is rather speed and ease of connection – the quality of public transport – which define our experience and perception of distance.

In this sense the aerotropolis idea is flawed: it fails to acknowledge the relative nature of movement within cities, and that although we may be very flexible about how (and how far) we move from one activity to another, we are less flexible about our need for a good environment with which we can truly connect; a place where we can feel at home.

References

1 Francesco di Giorgio Martini, *Trattato di Architettura, Ingegneria e Arte Militare*, 1485, quoted by Spiro Kostof in *The City Shaped: Urban Patterns and Meanings through History*, Thames & Hudson (London), 1991, p 52.

2 W Boesiger and H Girsberger, *Le Corbusier 1910–65*, Les Éditions d'Architecture (Zurich), 1967, p 320.

3 Le Corbusier, *The City of To-morrow and its Planning* [*Urbanisme* [1924], 8th edition, 1929], translated by Frederick Etchells, Dover Publications (New York), 1987, p 278.

4 *Ibid*.

5 *Ibid* pp 280–81.

6 *Ibid*.

7 Alain de Botton, *The Architecture of Happiness*, Penguin Books (London), 2007, p 240.

8 Le Corbusier called the Modulor 'a harmonic measure to the human scale': see Boesiger and Girsberger, p 291. See also Chapter 6.

9 Francesco di Giorgio Martini, *Trattato di Architettura, Ingegneria e Arte Militare*, 1485, quoted in Kostof, *The City Shaped*, p 52.

10 Jan Gehl, *Cities for People*, Island Press (Washington, DC; Covelo, CA; and London), 2010, p 38. Gehl speaks more of urban spaces than of street widths or block dimensions.

11 Steve Mouzon, 'Walk Appeal', 24 July 2012, *Original Green* blog, http://www.originalgreen.org/blog/walk-appeal.html [accessed 4 April 2014].

12 Christopher Alexander, Sara Ishikawa, Murray Silverstein, Max Jacobson, Ingrid Fiksdahl-King and Shlomo Angel, *A Pattern Language: Towns, Buildings, Construction*, Oxford University Press (New York),

1977, p 64.

13 Anne Bransford, 'The Development Battle', Covent Garden Memories website, 7 November 2012, http://www.coventgardenmemories.org.uk [accessed 4 April 2014].

14 Robert Wright, 'Metro system: Neighbours keep close eye on success of Dubai scheme', *Financial Times*, 8 April 2011.

15 'Hollande veut faire le non-cumul des mandats dans le quinquennat', *Le Monde*, 16 January 2013 (author's translation).

16 Nicolai Ouroussoff, 'Remaking Paris', *New York Times*, 8 June 2009.

17 Edward Glaeser, *Triumph of the City*, Pan Macmillan (London), 2011.

18 JH Forshaw and Patrick Abercrombie, County of London Plan, Macmillan and Co Ltd for London County

Council, 1943.

19 Søren Aabye Kierkegaard (1813–1855) writing to his niece Henriette Lund in 1847, quoted by Jan Gehl in *Cities for People*, p V.

20 Msheireb is the 35-hectare (86-acre) mixed-use development in the centre of Old Doha, being developed by Msheireb Properties, subsidiary of Qatar Foundation. The name means 'place of sweet water' because this land had good wells. It was therefore chosen as the best place to build new houses when Doha began to grow after World War Two.

21 Jane Jacobs, *The Death and Life of Great American Cities* [1961], Vintage Books (New York), 1992, p 178, Chapter 9 on 'The Need for Small Blocks', Condition 2.

22 *ICT Facts and Figures: The World in 2013*, ICT Data and Statistics Division, International Telecommunications Union (Geneva), February 2013, http://www.itu.int/en/ITU-D/Statistics/Documents/facts/ICTFactsFigures2013-e.pdf [accessed 30 April 2014].

23 Patricia Reaney, 'Most of world interconnected through email, social media', Reuters, 27 March 2012, http://www.reuters.com/article/2012/03/27/net-us-socialmedia-online-poll-idUSBRE82Q0C420120327 [accessed 30 April 2014].

24 *Compact Oxford English Dictionary*, 2nd edition, Oxford University Press (Oxford), 1992.

25 See 'U.S. online spending on Cyber Monday from 2005 to 2013 (in million U.S. dollars)', Statista, 4 December 2013, http://www.statista.com/statistics/194643/us-e-commerce-spending-on-cyber-monday-since-2005/ [accessed 30 April 2014].

26 Tim Begany, 'Is Online Shopping Killing Brick-and-Mortar?', *Investopedia*, 28 July 2011.

27 'Skype: The most popular video calling application on Android', Skype Big Blog, 25 June 2012 (from Google Play June 2012 data), http://blogs.skype.com/2012/0 [accessed 30 April 2014]

28 Gwyn Topham, 'Heathrow airport passes 70m passenger milestone', *The Guardian*, 11 April 2012.

29 IATA Press Release 28, 30 May 2013.

30 John D Kasarda and Greg Lindsay, *The Evolution of Airport Cities and the Aerotropolis*, Insight Media (London), 2008.

31 John D Kasarda and Greg Lindsay, *Aerotropolis: The Way We'll Live Next*, Allen Lane (London), 2011, p 287.

3
On Scale
and Edges

'In narrow streets and small spaces, we can see buildings, details and the people around us at close range. There is so much to assimilate, buildings and activities abound and we experience them with great intensity.'

Jan Gehl, *Cities for People*, 2010[1]

In the two preceding chapters we have considered firstly how we experience cities in time: over years, decades and generations, as they grow and shrink and grow again; how their history, far beyond our own lifespan, is nonetheless part of our immediate and everyday experience. Secondly, we have examined how we experience cities through movement from one place to another, where the dimensions of our perception include time, information and mode of travel, as well as distance and geometry. This chapter moves on to discuss our experience of spaces within cities: enclosures between buildings, distances we can see with our eyes, volumes we can feel with our bodies.

In Chapter 2, the second thesis of the book was posed (see page 50); that there are universal norms of scale in the making of cities, which all people hold broadly in common and against which all relativities can be judged. Even if it is impossible to define these precisely, they are rules of thumb and we should not feel shy or unqualified in saying 'feels too big' or 'looks out of scale' or 'not big enough'. Remembering the child under the table, there is within us all both a child and a giant: two beings with finely attuned and largely unconscious senses of scale who simply want to feel at home in the city, whether in their house or apartment (under the table), in their castle in the sky, or out on the street.

Far Too Far

There are three cities, notable for their excessive scale, which can be seen as examples of the over-scaled city. All of them, perhaps not surprisingly, are capital cities created in accordance with a grand plan: Chandigarh, Abuja and Washington.

Travelling through Chandigarh, on a brief stop on the way to the mountains, the words of my rickshaw driver while driving from the station to the Capitol have stayed with me: 'very clean and neat this city, plenty of space'. We seemed to drive forever along avenues which felt too wide to know where we were or understand where we were going, but we did eventually arrive at Le Corbusier's Indian masterpiece: the Capitol Complex built from 1951 to 1959 under Nehru's leadership, to establish the new state capital for the eastern Punjab after Partition in 1947, when the western side became part of Pakistan, including the former capital, Lahore. The space between

Le Corbusier, High Court, Capitol Complex, Chandigarh, 1955
The architecture is scaled to the landscape but the spaces between buildings seem over-scaled in relation to people.

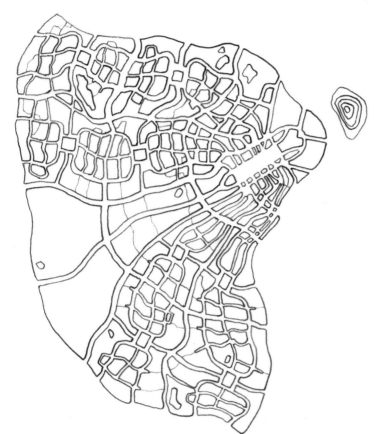

Sketch (2014) by the
author after Kenzo
Tange's 1978 plan for
Abuja
The axial plan is focused on
Aso Rock. Organic 'veins'
spread out from the central
spine.

these buildings measures almost half a kilometre (a third of a mile) and, in
spite of the grandeur of the architecture, their masterly composition and
exceptional use of sculptural muscle, this overly spacious piazza made me feel
small; it sapped my energy. Le Corbusier's vast hand sculpture, seen against
the backdrop of the mountains, could not be a more poignant reminder
of the human touch running throughout his work, sometimes guided and
sometimes misguided, but in this case it seemed too distant. The hand is truly
immense when one arrives at it, and it is certainly a strong presence on the
horizon, but one has to ask: would the space of the Capitol Complex and the
parts played by the individual components, including the hand, be improved
if they were all brought closer together?

Tulip leaf
The structure of the leaf is delineated by layers of veins: large, medium and small.

Abuja, the new capital of Nigeria established in 1991 on an empty savannah midway between the Muslim North and the Christian South, is a city with an intriguing plan, originally drawn up by Kenzo Tange, with Wallace Roberts & Todd, in 1978. It has a 'Beaux-Arts' axial core, from which flows an organic street pattern, like the interconnecting lines of the veins on the underside of the tulip leaf (pictured) which I brought back as a souvenir from a trip there in 2005. Rather than having a central axis, there are two spines, one related to the central mosque and the other to the cathedral. On the centre line, far in the distance but vast on the horizon, is Aso Rock, a great sugar-loaf of granite which stands as a symbol of universal nature, neither Christian nor Muslim; very powerful but impossibly far away. The plan is beautiful, the conception is beautiful but the spaces of the city, whether experienced from a car or on foot, are not. The scale is twice what it should be to enable people to feel at home. It is a city disconnected by highways and over-scaled distance, despite the genius of its plan and the benign magnificence of Aso Rock. Were these new capitals scaled up, beyond what is comfortable, in order to allow room for growth, as in L'Enfant's statement on Washington – 'to leave room for aggrandizement'[2] – or was it because simple big-ness is seen as synonymous with power? When laying out a new city, is it an almost impossible form of enlightenment and self-control to achieve a sense of intimacy in the distances between things? Christopher Alexander asks the same question: 'Time and

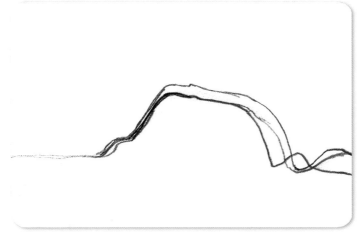

Aso Rock, Abuja
Abuja's 400-metre-high (1,300-foot) granite monolith is visible from all over the city but if one tries to reach it, it seems impossibly far away.

again in modern cities, architects and planners build plazas that are too large. They look good on drawings; but in real life they end up desolate and dead.'[3] Surprisingly Le Corbusier agrees with him, in theory if not in practice: 'when man finds himself alone in vast empty spaces he grows disheartened. We must learn how to tighten up the urban landscape and discover units of measurement to our own scale.'[4]

The central spine of Washington is an extreme case of distances which are not only excessive but also deceptive. Washington, although its position as a capital city is more ancient and more deeply rooted than Abuja or Chandigarh, is perhaps once again a case of size being used to compensate for a lack of true scale. It is not naturally located for a capital, nor is it an obvious choice economically, demographically or culturally for such a role. It is only the 24th largest city in America, its population being less than a tenth of New York's. This is the background to a city which, even if room for future growth was one of the factors in its conception, seems to have been designed with a sense of over-scaled monumentalism, at the expense of successful urban realm. Looking along the Mall from Capitol Hill towards the Washington Monument, the great obelisk, which at 170 metres (560 feet) is the world's tallest stone structure, is of a scale which makes it feel reachable. It is in fact some 2 kilometres (over a mile) away. This would not be so far if we were not expecting something much closer. As one walks towards it, time seems to stand still; space is defied. One feels it cannot be too far, but it gets no closer. When one eventually arrives at the obelisk, at the end of a seemingly eternal walk, it is indeed monumental in scale; but its relationships to its surroundings, to people and to distance are illusory. At this point, scale and size part company.

City Carved

Despite the immensity of the axial components of America's monumental strip, with the Capitol to the east and the Lincoln Memorial to the west, separated by 3.5 kilometres (more than two miles) of distance, it is the edges on either side which define space, with less rather than more success. The edges of the Washington Mall feel weak compared with the grand frontages of Central Park in New York or Michigan Avenue in Chicago. The necessity to give strong definition and appropriate scale – proportion – to urban edges should be a preoccupation of designers. It lies at the heart of meeting our expectations of scale – the means by which we experience size – and helping

Robert Mills, Washington Monument, 1884
The super-scale of the obelisk makes it seem closer than it really is.

ESSEX
HOUSE

JULY 4 '13

us to feel at home in the city, to gauge it, to touch or connect with it, both in private and public places.

In Central Park, in spite of the fact that it is all too easy to feel quite lost there, on account of Frederick Law Olmsted's exaggeratedly naturalistic layout of paths, lakes and plantings,[5] originally conceived to give a 'sense of space' but to some extent achieving the reverse; notwithstanding this, the clarity of the wall of buildings surrounding the Park – Fifth Avenue, 59th Street, Central Park West, richly diverse in its skyline and texture but clear and strong in its geometry and bold in its height – is exemplary. This is a case where big buildings, following clear lines (straight or otherwise), can successfully give enclosure to big spaces in cities, in ways which lower buildings cannot do. A sense of enclosure, at large or small scale, brings both intimacy and grandeur, which cities thrive on in equal measure.

Granary Square – at the heart of the King's Cross masterplan[6] for Argent by Porphyrios Associates and Allies and Morrison, where I was fortunate to be the project director and then partner – although smaller than Central Park, is a good example of the value of strong edges: large for large and

Central Park, New York: drawing by the author, 4 July 2013
The buildings surrounding Central Park are well scaled in relation to the great space of the park.

small for small. Now under construction between the Midland and Great Northern railway lines on the north side of central London, King's Cross is a large mixed-use development with a 6-hectare (15-acre) urban park at its centre: the historic Goods Yard, threaded through the middle by the ribbon-like Regent's Canal. At the centre of the Goods Yard sits Granary Square. On one side of the square sits the mighty Granary Building, designed by Lewis Cubitt in 1851 as the focus of the world's first multi-modal transport hub, connecting road, rail and canal. In those days the space in front of the building was a canal basin rather than a square and three channels entered under the building for sacks of grain to be loaded directly to and from the barges and trains. On the other side a phalanx of large new masterplan blocks is rising, offices for Google, BNP Paribas and others. Between these sits the diminutive Fish & Coal Building, a waif-like sliver following the northern curve of the Canal. Built at the same time as the Granary Building, it is on an altogether smaller scale than the great blocks which surround it.[7]

Granary Square is a space within a space: a space 90 metres (300 feet) wide – the same size as Leicester Square – within a space 150 metres (500 feet) wide – the same size as Trafalgar Square, one of London's largest. Both spaces

Granary Square, King's Cross, London, during redevelopment in 2014
The inner layer of enclosure is created by the four-storey Fish & Coal Building (1851). Beyond it the 12-storey office buildings of Goods Way define the space of the square as a whole.

are strongly contained by built edges which give them a room-like quality, as if the space has been carved. If the outer layer – the large buildings on the south side of the Canal – were less tall, then the urban space of Granary Square would be less successful. There are some who argue that the new 12-storey buildings 'loom' over the Canal and 'dwarf' the four-storey Fish & Coal Building. However these critics are fixated on size and are failing to remember that scale is relative. In the case of Granary Square, scale is about relationships between foreground and background, between inner and outer, and in terms of character, between future and past.

The big space of Granary Square, which at the design stage people worried might feel desolate and windswept, positively benefits from the muscular scale of its containing walls – to make it feel habitable, in spite of its size. The big buildings make the space feel smaller in a positive way, and being there is a 'larger than life' experience. For urban spaces, height and width are relative, so too are quantities and qualities. King's Cross is a place of contrasts; it has a strong spirit, and the thunderous muscle of the 19th-century railway pioneers who built it is felt side by side with the almost rural charm of the Canal and St Pancras Lock. This duality is essential to both the scale and the feeling of this place; it is where the tangible and the intangible meet. To return for a moment to Central Park or the Washington Mall, too much space is not a good thing; nor is lack of definition. Strong edges can make a large space feel splendid.

Liquid Space

In his chapter on 'Intimate Immensity' in *The Poetics of Space*, Gaston Bachelard extends his thinking from the preceding chapter, 'Miniature', by pondering the grandeur of the 'intimate forest'[8] which can be seen as a metaphor for the city. From there he zooms in on the interior of a tree filled with viscous, honey-like space, to release 'the expansion of infinite things'. There is an analogy here with our physical experience of space, both ordinary and extraordinary, both internal and external. An urban space, large or small, is something we inhabit; it has substance. We experience it through a process of compression and expansion, both literally – tall narrow spaces, wide open spaces – and by empathy or projection, with our eyes, our mind and our heart. We experience it both at our own size, and through our feelings and imagination, at sizes larger and smaller than ourselves. This is a scale-ratio and a clue to being comfortable in the city. The interior nature of the city – its inner sweetness – is something which can be unlocked, revealed or simply made the most of by its inhabitants, if the city is treated as a continuum of interior spaces.

The importance of defined urban edges giving containment to urban space is well illustrated by a comparison between the streets of Doha's West Bay and downtown Abu Dhabi. West Bay has been developing at high speed since the 1990s, on a piece of landfill forming the northern edge of Doha Bay. Seen from a distance, it has now reached maturity as a piece of city. Its skyline is now an essential part of Doha's identity; it is integral to the city's defining motif, the elliptical curve of Doha Bay which sets up a strong dialogue across the water between the new and old parts of the city centre. From within however, West Bay is unfinished business. It is not only difficult to navigate, as mentioned in Chapter 2, but it lacks clarity in terms of urban space. Plots have been developed with a seemingly random scattering of towers, each with large set-backs given over to car parking. It is like an accidental still-life strewn on a table. The buildings stand as objects, drawing attention to themselves with a pot-pourri of shapes and surface graphics, while the spaces between buildings are residual, left-over spaces, rather than being defined in any positive way. Standing in a street in West Bay – closing one's eyes, then opening them again – one can imagine urban space as a kind of

West Bay, Doha
The glass and metal towers sit isolated from each other. The spaces between them are left over and the environment for pedestrians is hostile.

tangible liquid, but in this case one feels it leaking away before it is ever allowed to settle. Added to this the widths of the streets, and the lack of shade or any form of welcoming or cohesive frontage, all contribute to a sense of alienation.

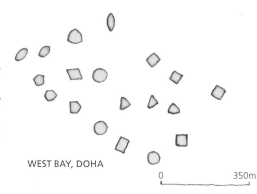

WEST BAY, DOHA

0   350m

Urban Edges, figure-ground of Doha, 2014
The figure-ground of West Bay Doha – objects in space, compared with London's West End – carved urban blocks; both at the same scale.

Object buildings with leftover space

In contrast to this, Abu Dhabi's downtown area does benefit from clearly defined street edges, even though the majority of individual buildings are of mediocre quality at best, like so many of the recent boom towns around the world. The Abu Dhabi grid has created a pattern of urban blocks, where

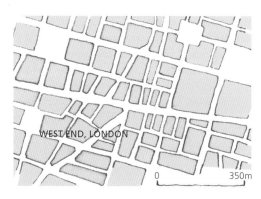

WEST END, LONDON

0   350m

Urban blocks with space defined

the street wall, made up of many buildings touching, makes the streets into clear spaces. On the interior of the blocks, urban squares – currently car parks which it is easy to imagine being transformed into people-friendly public gardens – form positive volumes, albeit on a very large scale. In neither case are the buildings modest in height or the streets sufficiently narrow to cross with ease. However the example of Abu Dhabi (or New York or Chicago) is that buildings that stand shoulder to shoulder, making a strong street wall, and are of sufficient height in relation to the width of the spaces they address, are establishing a basis for a sense of scale within the city. Public space is the positive, to which buildings form the backdrop. Public spaces are like carved solids, or castings to which buildings form the mould.

Many car-bound months spent in West Bay (except for the time I experimented with a foldable bike and was knocked down while walking

Central Park as seen from the Rockefeller Center, Midtown New York
The strong clear edge of the park is carved out of the urban fabric.

it across a pedestrian crossing when the green man was green)[9] led me to study how a street such as this might be transformed over time by adding a layer of enclosure, giving definition to the space of the street, introducing an intermediary scale and creating a degree of comfort through crossings, arcades and active street frontage. As well as both rescaling and humanising the city, a transformation such as this could bring a degree of harmony to an otherwise disparate place.

Makower Architects, Retro-Fit City, a vision for Doha's Central Business District, 2012
West Bay could be transformed by the addition of urban edges, making streets narrower and easier to cross, creating shade, and introducing active street edges with welcoming cafés, shops and entrance lobbies to replace surface car parks.

Doha, photographed in 1947
The old town of Doha, dating back more than a century, is made of 'carved urban clay'. Buildings give enclosure to public space.

Stitching the City

I have given up staying in West Bay now. I prefer Old Doha where I can cross the road to buy milk before walking to work, just 15 minutes away. The remaining fragments of the old city around my hotel are a reminder of the 'carved city' of the past and in many ways the Msheireb masterplan, mentioned in the previous chapter, emulates its qualities. Not only is Msheireb a set piece of 'carved urbanism', with strong edges made up of multiple buildings touching each other, but it also has achieved narrow streets, which are so important for creating shade and easy crossings, in a way which is not found in other parts of Doha. Street widths are often dictated just as much by the requirements of utility companies as by traffic loads, because all the underground pipes must be laid side by side, with generous space, so that they can be accessed from above for maintenance, by digging trenches in the road. This makes them so wide that they are almost impossible to cross, particularly in summer. In a masterplan such as Msheireb, where all utilities are housed in a labyrinth of underground tunnels, and traffic is reduced to the absolute minimum, narrow streets become a possibility. This, combined with the density of medium-rise buildings (six to 12 storeys across most of the site), has enabled the re-proportioning of streets to something more akin to the pre-car city, although on a much larger scale.

At Home in the City

Leon Battista Alberti's timeless words quoted in the Introduction[10] to this book remind us firstly that cities are made up of urban rooms, large and small, interconnected and capable of both function and beauty, like the rooms of a house. Secondly, that they will be more likely to succeed if they are conceived in a sense as indoor spaces, and their proportions – height to length to breadth – are judged as positive volumes, even though urban spaces are often far larger than any interior room. Thirdly, they affirm the fact that cities are for people to dwell in, and the boundaries between indoors and outdoors, between public and private realms, continually overlap.

Giambattista Nolli's seminal plan of Rome from 1748, where the interiors of all public buildings are continuous with the streets,[11] illustrates Alberti's point. As we navigate the plan, moving our finger across the hand-etched map, we find the modelled piazzetta of Santa Maria della Pace, transforming a residual space into a larger-than-life vestibule within the city. We move to the carved Piazza Sant'Ignazio, the meeting of small alleyways shaped into oval voids, in dialogue with the church facade opposite, and then we arrive at the perfectly scaled Piazza della Rotonda, the 'salone' of the Campus Martius.

The delightful square of the Pantheon, Agrippa's temple to many gods, originally built around 30 BC and reconstructed by Hadrian around AD 125, is old and its memory can be felt in every stone. The space is thought to have begun life in Roman times as a rectangular colonnaded courtyard, designed to frame the temple portico and completely to conceal the fact that the space within was circular, until the moment of coming through its inner doorway.[12] The square was cleared of medieval accretions in the 1430s, further rationalised as a formal piazza in the 17th century, and in the early 19th century narrowly escaped becoming a greatly enlarged node of several grand boulevards, under Napoleon's rule. Like a drawing room hung with a collection of paintings from different times and places, its windows and the inscribed plaques around its walls tell stories. I sit and read. My neighbour, an aged academic with thick glasses, slowly turns through his papers, waiting for a young friend. A waiter at the next café struggles with an umbrella, a man and a woman in dressing gowns look down from a window above.

This is a large outdoor sitting room, with the sky for a ceiling. Clusters of people group themselves, sitting at the cafés, and milling about; some are

090

Nolli's plan of Rome, 1748
The streets and spaces of the
city are shown as part of a
'carved continuum' together
with all public buildings.

moving in Brownian motion, interacting, never meeting; others rest in the shade, static but animating the space with a quiet babble of voices and ringtones. Two bicycles pass through and a bell cuts the air. The piazza is hard-paved, with no trees, but it is softened by all this life. The light and colour from west to east grades from blue to gold; from the canvas awnings and tablecloths in cool shade, to the walls of the houses in warm sunlight; yellow, cream and grey. The satin reflections on the cobbles, burnished over centuries, make the paving into a carpet. The plaques on the Albergo del Sole opposite tell me that Pietro Mascagni, composer of *Cavalleria Rusticana*, stayed here in 1890 and, 377 years earlier, Ludovico Ariosto, writer of *Orlando Furioso*[13] and sometimes said to be Titian's 'man with a quilted sleeve', had stayed here in the spring. From which window might he have looked out onto the square, all those years ago, I wonder?

These walls, laden with narrative, are the walls of an 'outdoor room'. When buildings touch each other, sharing party walls, they cease to be object-like. They become part of something larger than themselves – an urban block, an urban edge, an urban space. This is the clay from which the city is carved. Cities cannot cohere, and public spaces will not acquire positive form without being enclosed by facades which touch, or nearly touch. At this moment a 'figure-ground reversal' occurs.[14] The 'figure', what was the solid volume

Piazza della Rotonda,
Rome
Stone plaques around the
Piazza della Rotonda hold
layers of narrative.

of the building, becomes the 'ground' – in other words the backdrop or background to an open space; the space between buildings is formed. The facades of buildings which touch are no longer the skin of a building so much as they are the enclosing shell of a void. 'Void' however is a misleading term. The Piazza della Rotonda is anything but void. It is full.

The piazza is full in every sense of the word; it is furnished. How can we feel at home in the city if we cannot furnish the rooms of our house? In an apartment looking out onto the Rotonda, the world does not stop at the window, the balcony or the front door. The boundaries are blurred between inner and outer worlds, private and public. Our experience of the city is continuous; a continuity of many layers; a complexity of many sensations. The Piazza della Rotonda, like so many successful rooms within the city, is full of layers, in time and space, sound and smell. Its times of day, its constituent parts, permanent and temporary, its colours and light, its movements, activities and events, its narratives and memories – some explicit, some implicit – make it what it is.

Outdoor Rooms

The other significant aspect of the Piazza della Rotonda is its proportion. It is approximately 60 metres (200 feet) square, although it widens on the east

Place Nationale, Montauban
A well-proportioned outdoor room.

Place du Capitole, Toulouse
Too wide an expanse in proportion to the scale of its edges.

side, creating a theatrical 'wing', like a stage in front of the Pantheon. The vertical faces of the buildings, which vary in height around the square, are less than half its width but are sufficiently tall to assert themselves and give positive enclosure to the outdoor room.

So can spaces succeed or fail on account of their proportion? A comparison between the Place du Capitole in Toulouse and the Place Nationale in Montauban provides an answer. Each space is surrounded by four-storey buildings. The square in Montauban is 40 by 50 metres (130 by 160 feet) and the buildings are about a third as high as the space is wide. Founded in the 12th century and reconstructed as a unified classical composition in the mid-17th century, its cornices frame the sky, like the cornices of a grand salon framing the ceiling. It invites people to make themselves at home in the city; enjoy being in this space, take a seat at the edge or come into the centre, join with the band and dance.

By contrast, the space in Toulouse is 90 by 120 metres (290 by 390 feet) and the height of the buildings is about one eighth of its width. Originally the city's Roman forum, reconstructed in the 18th century in cold classical

Place Nationale arcades,
Montauban
The double arcades in
Montauban cater both for
movement and for people
sitting at tables.

style, it is a vast open acreage, unwelcoming to cross and impossible to inhabit. Activity clings to its edges and lurks in its arcades, but even these are awkwardly proportioned. Although the square is far too large, in proportion to the height of its edges, ironically its arcades are too narrow. They are only 3 metres (10 feet) wide – too tight to be occupied with café tables while allowing any space to walk, in the shade or out of the rain. Montauban on the other hand has one of the best arcades in France. On all four sides of the square there are double arcades, with the outer, narrower vault being used for café tables and the inner, wider one for movement. The clear width of each is about the same as at Toulouse, but they are lower in proportion to the space they surround, achieving both generosity and intimacy at the same time, as well as better shade and shelter. It is an obvious paradox that the lesser space (Montauban) can feel like more, and the greater space (Toulouse) can feel like less.

Jan Gehl in his *Cities for People* makes clear-cut observations about what a good size for a square is, but he does not talk about its proportion – the relation of its width to its height. His recommendation that squares should generally not be larger than 80 by 100 metres (260 by 330 feet) is based on human sight – to achieve the 'best of two worlds: overview and detail'[15] – rather than on spatial qualities. As is indicated by the opening quote to

Place du Capitole arcades,
Toulouse (opposite page)
The arcades in Toulouse are
too narrow to accommodate
café seating and a walking
route.

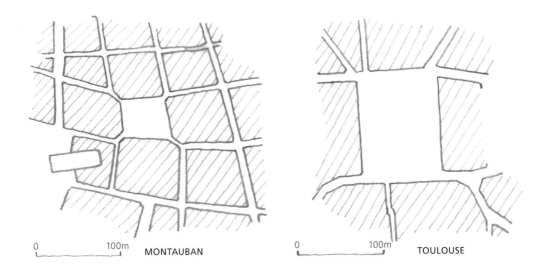

0 ___ 100m   MONTAUBAN

0 ___ 100m   TOULOUSE

this chapter, Gehl is driven by a highly enlightened sense of the importance of intimacy and intensity in cities but he sometimes fails to acknowledge the value of grandeur. Christopher Alexander goes even further. In his chapter on 'Small Public Squares', he observes that 'for some reason there is a temptation to make these public squares too large'[16] and goes on to recommend a maximum dimension of 25 metres (80 feet) for a successful public space. By all standards this is small, and depending on its context it may be too small. One of London's best-proportioned public spaces, and least known, is Soho's Golden Square, near Piccadilly Circus. It is a simple rectangular space and its edges, which are diverse in terms of width and height of frontage, and architectural character, hold the space beautifully. At 65 by 65 metres (210 by 210 feet), it is halfway between Gehl's and Alexander's paradigms.

The notion of the urban room is well represented by the three mid-sized squares we have examined in Rome, Montauban and London. The lines of a plan, when extruded into three dimensions, become street-walls: the shell which gives enclosure to 'carved' urban space, the backdrop of our lives. This is the interior of the city to which we belong, as our home belongs to us. A city is indeed like a house. Its streets are its corridors; its piazzas are its rooms. It is the job of a city to be a home for people; and homeliness, on an urban scale, is not easy to achieve.

Scale comparison between Place Nationale in Montauban (left) and Place du Capitole in Toulouse (right): drawings by the author, 2014 Room-like compactness compared with too much space, or not enough enclosure.

Golden Square, Soho, London
An urban space of 65 metres (210 feet) square, well enclosed by strong but diverse edges.

The importance of scale is not as a set of absolutes with which to comply, but as a framework from which to establish (and feel) relationships: a framework of connections between people and places, between indoors and outdoors, between large and small. This chapter is as much in praise of big-ness as small-ness. The aim, for the giant and the child in us all, is to be able to reach out and 'touch' those things which are usually considered to be out of reach, and to feel a sense of belonging; in Bachelard's words, 'the better I am at miniaturising the world, the better I possess it'.[17]

In this chapter, as well as examining the qualitative aspects of urban edges, and how they relate to large and small spaces, we have touched on the difference between solid and void, object and edge. As a case study on this point, it is interesting to contemplate the three incarnations of Ground Zero, formerly known as 'Radio Row' and then the World Trade Center, in Lower Manhattan. It was an area, before its demolition in the 1970s, comprising 12 urban blocks, each one in turn made up of numerous buildings, all touching. In the latter decade, it became the site of the Twin Towers (by Minoru Yamasaki, 1972) which briefly became the tallest buildings in

America. These buildings were vast and object-like. As urban blocks of 55 metres (180 feet) square, they were not too large to navigate around by foot – something which, at 150 metres (490 feet) across, the Burj Khalifa in Dubai (by Skidmore, Owings & Merrill, 2010) certainly is. However as singular objects they contradicted the space which surrounded them, to create a windswept and desolate place, inhospitable to people. Each tower would have fitted neatly into Golden Square; their footprint was not their problem. Together however the two towers were achieving the reverse of creating successful outdoor rooms, not because of their height but because of their uncompromising object-quality, and their problematic scale-ratio to context. At the heart of the question of scale-ratio lies not dimension, nor proportion, but the 'texture of human activity' – the patina of higgledy-piggledy human life which makes itself at home at the edges of buildings. It is a patina which, in contrast to the vernacular blocks of Radio Row, the Twin Towers firmly denied.

Radio Row, Downtown Manhattan, New York, photographed in 1930
The site of the World Trade Center was once a 'fine-grain' area of streets and urban blocks. It then became the site of two of the world's largest objects, which have now been replaced by two voids.

Ground Zero, New York
The two fountains at Ground Zero are a monumental statement of loss, on the scale of the events of 11 September 2001.

In the words of Paul Randour, who spent many a day and night in the area of Radio Row in the pre-World Trade Center days:

> Yes it was shabby but it used to have a good feel, there were some nice streets with cafés – that's where we used to go for lunch. Building the World Trade Center was the first time the area was destroyed; it became a dead place after that; it lost its soul. With the arrival of the Twin Towers, all I remember was garbage blowing around and emptiness.[18]

To visit Ground Zero today is a desolate experience in a different way. The scale of the blackened voids, gushing with a sheer quantity of water and noise which is truly hard to describe, seeks to make for a memorial in scale with the events of 9/11, if that were ever possible. The fact that the exact footprints of the two towers are now deep voids, so deep that one cannot see where the water vanishes to, is a lesson in scale and is far from the ordinary. It is a troubled place of memory. Its prevailing characteristics today are those of emptiness and monumentality. For reasons which are understandable, it lacks the qualities of urban enclosure and 'habitable edges' with which this chapter is primarily concerned.

References

1 Jan Gehl, *Cities for People*, Island Press (Washington, DC; Covelo, CA; and London), 2010, p 53.

2 See Chapter 1, section on 'Centredness' and note 4.

3 Christopher Alexander, Sara Ishikawa, Murray Silverstein, Max Jacobson, Ingrid Fiksdahl-King and Shlomo Angel, *A Pattern Language: Towns, Buildings, Construction*, Oxford University Press (New York), 1977, section 61 on Small Public Squares, p 310.

4 Le Corbusier, *The City of To-morrow and its Planning* [*Urbanisme* [1924], 8th edition, 1929], translated by Frederick Etchells, Dover Publications (New York), 1987, p 237.

5 The design for Central Park was won in competition by FL Olmsted and Calvert Vaux in 1858.

6 The King's Cross development by Argent is a 27-hectare (67-acre) masterplan, now half complete, comprising 750,000 square metres (8 million square feet) of space for office, retail, residential, culture and education. There are 10 hectares (25 acres) of public space with numerous listed heritage buildings around the former Goods Yard and the Regent's Canal.

7 The Fish & Coal Building, built in 1851, gained its name simply because the trade in those two commodities was managed from this building. It adjoined the Stone and Coal Basin.

8 Gaston Bachelard, *The Poetics of Space* [*La Poétique de l'espace*, 1957], translated by Maria Jolas, Beacon Press (Boston, MA), 1969, pp 183 to 202 – quotes Rainer Maria Rilke, 'through every human being, unique space, intimate space, opens up to the world', and Joë Bousquet on 'the expansion of infinite things', 'Space is nowhere. Space is inside it like honey in a hive' (Bousquet, *La Neige d'un autre âge*, p 92).

9 Luckily I had my helmet on, so the car which hit me was dented rather than my head.

10 See Introduction, note 8.

11 Giambattista Nolli's plan was commissioned by Pope Benedict XIV to help determine boundaries for the 14 traditional *rioni* or districts of Rome.

12 John B Ward-Perkins, *Roman Architecture*, Faber and Faber (London) and Electa (Milan), 1974, p 93.

13 Pietro Mascagni, composer of *Cavalleria Rusticana* (1889). Ariosto, writer of *Orlando Furioso* (1516), was commander of the citadel of Canossa under Cardinal Ippolito d'Este.

14 The phrase 'figure-ground reversal' was used by Richard Serra when speaking at the Museum of Islamic Art, Doha at the unveiling of his sculpture *7* in 2010. Also of relevance is Colin Rowe's description of Le Corbusier's Unité d'Habitation in Marseilles (1952) as the reciprocal of Vasari's Uffizi Gallery in Florence (1581), one being the 'jelly mould' for the other: Colin Rowe and Fred Koetter, *Collage City*, MIT Press (Cambridge, MA), 1978, p 68.

15 Gehl, *Cities for People*, p 38.

16 Alexander *et al.*, *A Pattern Language*, p 311.

17 Bachelard, *The Poetics of Space*, p 150.

18 The author in conversation with Paul Randour, September 2013.

On Scale and Grain

4

'At the present tempo of building, there is not time for the slow adjustment of form to small, individualized forces. Therefore we must depend far more than formerly on conscious design: the deliberate manipulation of the world for sensuous ends.'

Kevin Lynch, *The Image of the City*, 1960[1]

Grain of growth
The long grain of timber indicates its direction of growth, the end grain denotes its age.

The grain of a piece of wood represents both its age and its direction of growth. The same is true of sedimentary stones; they build up in layers over time. If we look at a cut tree trunk, each ring marks out a year: winter to spring, spring to summer, summer to autumn, autumn to winter and round again. Faster-growing trees have a coarser grain because the rings are further apart. Slower-growing trees have

Lexington Street, Soho, London
A collage of vertical and horizontal grain. In the right foreground is the start of the long ribbon windows of Lexington House, a 1920s office building, contrasting with the upright nature of its 18th-century neighbours.

a finer grain. The laws of construction dictate that a timber column will be cut on the long grain. This is the direction of the tree as it grows up towards sunlight and forms its line of strength in bending. The rings of the tree are concentric cylinders and the end grain is revealed where the timber is cut. The differences between long grain and end grain, fine grain and coarse grain, as well as the fact that trees take time to grow, are analogous with the fabric and nature of cities.

Jigsaws and Patchworks

Lexington Street in Soho is an ordinary London street. On the west side is a line of houses, all built in the 18th century. One imagines each building being lived in by a merchant or shop-owner, proudly displaying his wares at street level and living above the shop. On the east side is Lexington House, a medium-sized 1920s office building built in the modernist Art Deco style of the day. The older buildings are between 7 and 12 metres (23 and 39 feet) wide, the newer is 35 metres (115 feet). The difference between them, in terms of size, breadth and the 'urban grain' of the street, reflects a natural process of expansion. As the city grows, so do its constituent parts. The city is made of increasingly large-size pieces; the grain becomes coarser over time while the process of change accelerates.

The narrower houses in Lexington Street are vertical in proportion and their multiple windows are also vertical, arranged in horizontal lines of two or three. The wider office building is dominated by a single long horizontal ribbon window at each storey, reflecting the open-plan flexible space within and emphatically celebrating its newness and the spread of the interior space, in contrast to the older buildings in the street. The fact that buildings of such difference coexist on this street is essential to its character. It is part of the 'happy hotchpotch' of London. However, if the buildings were all of the scale

A natural process of enlargement: drawing by the author, 2014
Urban blocks which begin as patchworks of small buildings, with a fine urban grain, gradually evolve into a coarser grain of larger elements.

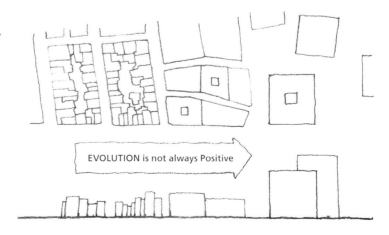

EVOLUTION is not always Positive

and proportion of Lexington House, it would be an entirely different place. It would have a coarser grain and would be more 'lumpy'.

No single landowner had control over this street; it was a patchwork of freehold ownerships from its earliest days. Land and buildings were developed as commodities through a natural economic process of maximising values and meeting the needs for increasingly large buildings. It is natural that buildings grow as the city grows, and it would be wrong to suppress the laws of supply and demand. This is the lifeblood and the pulse of the city and can lead to an unplanned but characterful diversity. In cases where estates comprising several urban streets and blocks together were developed under a single ownership, a very different character tends to be seen. Although large estates would always be broken down into phases of development, their speed and singularity of authorship tends towards greater unity, less diversity. This can produce either harmony or monotony. The notion of the 'masterplan' enters the frame.

Gower Street, Bedford Estate, Bloomsbury, London
A large-scale pattern of development but with some irregularities, reflecting its slow evolution over the course of the 18th century and enriching its character.

Lexington Street – a street without a masterplan – is like part of a jigsaw, made up of large and small pieces. In addition to the nature of ownerships and degrees of control over time being formative to its character, it is the sizing of the individual pieces of the jigsaw and the proportioning of facades along the street – both the overall dimensions and their subdivision into storeys, bays and openings – which define its character: its scale and grain.

The dukes, earls and viscounts of 18th-century London scaled up the jigsaw puzzle of the city to develop their prime pastures surrounding it with a new order. The squares of Grosvenor, Bedford and Portman, and other names to be conjured with, along with the surrounding streets, were in themselves unified – harmonised. These were developments, conceived with a comparable ambition to the dreams of post-war modernism, but on a scale happily limited by the times. The law of a competitive marketplace was the saviour of a city which, during the Georgian building boom, could have become oppressively homogeneous. Even a ducal masterplan was developed in smaller packages – a square here, a crescent there; six houses here, a full terrace there, as the market demanded – and the un-designed irregularities and differences between the pieces became enrichments, essential to its grain.

John Summerson remarks in his book *Georgian London*: 'London is remarkable for the freedom with which it developed. It is the city raised by private, not by public, wealth; the least authoritarian city in Europe.'[2] As we will see, the size of development parcels, speed of development and degrees of private or public control are fundamental factors in the 'scaling of the city', whether by a natural process of evolution or an imposed framework. If a city is to make a good place for people, these need to be treated as basics in the urban designer's toolkit, both at an economic and an experiential level.

New Order and the Dangers of Repetition

To fast-forward to more recent decades when mass housing became a pressing need for fast-growing cities, a visit to the World's End Estate in Chelsea is a challenge to the notion of urban grain. Since its early years it was associated with a dark side of the King's Road; punk rock, Vivienne Westwood's shop 'Sex' – with a large clock running backwards at high speed on the facade – and the sad story of someone who jumped from the top of one of the seven looming World's End towers. It is one of the most

Flashpoint

Blantyre

significant projects of Eric Lyons, the renowned designer of housing projects around London. Containing 750 apartments, it was finished between 1975 and 1977 and is a case study in scale. In many ways it is to be admired; it is sculptural, it encloses space with strongly formed edges, it balances the scale of the 17-storey towers with the lower blocks, wrapping the garden spaces. It is orientated towards the sun and the River Thames, and its layout is pleasingly non-rectilinear. Its fortress-like facades, made up of angles, balconies and bays, are subtly modulated from base to middle to top; and it creates a dramatic skyline, including the chimney stack, tied to the westernmost of the towers.

Its problem however, in spite of the intention 'to help minimize the feelings of "brutal monotony", "regimentation" and "lack of identity" [… and] relieve the impact of the "crushing scale" of the building when it is viewed from ground level',[3] is that it is monolithic in its conception. Even on a beautiful morning when the gardens are filled with the scent of cherry blossom, it becomes oppressive on account of its persistent repetition. Perhaps it would not take much to humanise it. If a project of this size – it is 200 metres (660 feet) across, covering 4 hectares (11 acres) – were to employ more than

Eric Lyons, World's End Estate, Chelsea, London, 1977: drawing by the author, 2014
Its looming towers were described in the *Architectural Review* at the time of its completion as a 'paraphrase of a medieval castle'.

World's End Estate
and Churchill Gardens,
Chelsea, compared
with Soho in London:
drawings by the author,
2014
The 20th-century Chelsea
estates are monolithic and
monotonous, in contrast
to the evolved urban grain
of Soho.

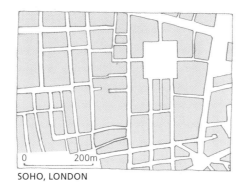

0   200m

SOHO, LONDON

0   200m

WORLD'S END

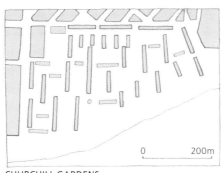

0   200m

CHURCHILL GARDENS

one colour of brick, or its facades, and the dwelling types within, had been designed using 'variations on a theme', perhaps it would have made a more friendly result; more scaled to the people who occupy it; more like places in cities which we know and love most.

If the architect were confronted with these thoughts, he may find them 'irrational'. He might reply, 'Why are you questioning a rigorous and well-honed solution? Why break a rational pattern if it is working well?' The answer is scale. A new definition of what is rational needs to be considered. Certain intuitive rules about size and scale, including the question of repetition in relation to people, need to be fed into the textbook, even if they are hard to put into words.

Not far from World's End, just along the river, lies Churchill Gardens – a pioneering housing scheme of 1,600 homes by architects Powell & Moya, developed between 1946 and 1962. Churchill Gardens is now designated as a conservation area and in the case of six of its marching rectangular nine-storey blocks (there are 32 blocks in all), together with its glass accumulator tower which recycled heat from Battersea Power Station on the opposite

side of the Thames to heat the estate, it was listed Grade II in 1990. The best of the blocks are very elegant and it is clearly a pleasant and comfortable place to live, partly because of its location in one of London's richest areas. However, covering an area of four times that of World's End – the same size as the centre of a typical market town, such as Marlborough in Wiltshire – it goes beyond what is a reasonable human scale for a piece of land under single ownership to be developed if a singular and repetitive architecture is to be employed. In spite of its heroism, it makes a person feel small.

A schoolboy on his way to school, when asked if he minded the repetition and if he ever found it hard to find his own front door, replied: 'You get used to it.'[4] A dress code is a good thing sometimes; it can lend harmony where there would otherwise be chaos, but at Churchill Gardens, the buildings are like battalions in uniform, more scary than schoolchildren. The project is unintentionally military in spirit and the inhabitants have to put up with it. Westminster City Council's Conservation Area Guide praises the project, saying 'the Estate achieves an overall integrity of design which is uncompromisingly modern for its time'.[5] Perhaps it would be more friendly if it were slightly more compromising.

Powell & Moya, Churchill Gardens, Chelsea, London, 1962
Repetitive linear blocks lack humanity of scale.

On Fine and Coarse Grain

To compare Churchill Gardens with the area surrounding Lexington Street
is to compare coarse with fine grain. Soho is a jigsaw puzzle, a 'fine-grain'
patchwork made of many fabrics stitched together. The 'coarse grain' of
Churchill Gardens, a project which has been lauded since it was first built
with phrases such as 'formally architectonic',[6] resides in three things. Firstly,
the area over which a consistent design and geometry have been applied
is too much. There is nothing wrong with a development being of this size,
or being developed over a short space of time, but this is too consistent,
too repetitive, to the point where it is oppressive and monotonous, even
if nicely designed. To those who disagree and say 'I think it is a good
design, it is rational and I like it, what's the problem?', the answer is that
opportunities have been missed to respond to human scale. There is a latent
need, and a delight, in us all for intimacy and a degree of complexity in
design – something which cannot be fully understood at a glance. Scale, in
this context, is one of the characteristics of a slow-grown city, or somewhere
which has the qualities of a place evolved over time, like a tree.

The second aspect of 'coarse grain' here at Churchill Gardens is the unbroken
linear length of the individual blocks. Buildings in the city can be gauged in
units of roughly 30 metres (100 feet); 30 is fine, 60 is okay, 90 is large and
120 is generally too large. Referring back to our second thesis (see page
50) – on the 'normative absolutes' of human scale – any piece of a city
designed beyond these dimensions without some degree of irregularity and
inconsistency being allowed or introduced will almost certainly fail to make
the most of opportunities for human comfort and delight. Is this a rational
proposition, is it rigorous? If it is good for people then it is rational. If it
applies to a sense of scale which most people have in common and can be
acknowledged as a universal guide, then it is surely rigorous.

The fact that Churchill Gardens was designed as a single project – a grand
and pioneering masterplan, a set piece of 'fast urbanism' – and represents
a 'rational' response to a brief for mass housing, is not a good reason for
failing to learn from, and emulate, some of what is best in our favourite
slow-grown cities. There is so much that is good about it, but nonetheless
it could be so much better in terms of urban scale and grain. Christopher
Alexander, in observing 'when a place is lifeless or unreal, there is almost
always a mastermind behind it. It is so filled with the will of its maker that

there is no room for its own nature',[7] is implying that the 'mastermind' is doomed to fail to create a 'real' place and one that is full of life, simply due to the singular scale of its conception, and perhaps the speed of its creation too. But he is overstating the case. It is not the fact of having a mastermind which is the problem; it is its approach. If the 'mastermind' is willing to pursue those characteristics in cities which make for the best places – large and small scale, regular and irregular – and to allow intuition to work in balance with intellect, then the best of both worlds is available: imposed order and evolved grain.

The third aspect of 'coarseness' at Churchill Gardens, worthy of consideration, is the separateness of the buildings from each other. They were forbidden to touch each other by the architects who, under the influence of Le Corbusier and others, would have come to the project with ideas of purity, cleanness and rigour – very understandable as a reaction to the violence, contortion and insanity of the World Wars. The blocks are freestanding rectangles, floating in a pure Cartesian space. They do give enclosure to external spaces to some extent on account of their linearity, but only loosely; the creation of habitable 'outdoor rooms' in the city – places to dwell – would have been far stronger if they had been allowed to nestle together. The buildings are strangely isolated and regimented at the same time; like a company of soldiers standing on parade, compared with a gathering of people in a piazza, huddling, chatting and milling about.

To have chosen a housing project which is undoubtedly a good piece of design in many respects, may be seen as a peculiar way to make a critical point; however, it has been chosen precisely because its failings are by no means commonly accepted and there are many in the field of urbanism today who would deny its negative aspects.

Urban Jazz

Is there a size for a piece of a city – a development, an urban block, a building or a facade – which is 'too big' or 'too small'? Are there degrees of repetition beyond which the quality of a project will diminish unless irregularity is consciously introduced? Rhythm is something we all respond to – regular or syncopated, fast or slow – but there are few who favour monotony. Are there rules of harmony which dictate that similarities between buildings, to greater or lesser degrees, can either enrich or detract

The 'projects' (housing schemes) of Lower East Side, New York
Several kilometres of monotonous brown brick blocks: a permanent bruise on the face of Manhattan.

from people's experience of the city? Would the answers to such questions differ in New York, London, Paris or Doha?

I embarked on a long-intended study in monotony last Independence Day in Lower Manhattan. 'The projects' – local authority housing developed mainly in the 1950s on the Lower East Side – are notorious for their massive repetitious blocks in bland brown brick; there are more than 100 of them, extending over 3 kilometres (nearly 2 miles) of the city with almost no variety. It was a blistering summer's day and there was a festive 4th July feel in the air, but nonetheless as I walked I felt my senses being gradually numbed, and abraded, by an overbearing coarseness of grain. In terms of their urban strategy, these blocks owe much to Le Corbusier, particularly their cruciform plan and gridded layout, and nowhere is this more strongly felt than driving along the East River. One can drive at speed for many minutes – it seems like 10 or 15 – all the way to the United Nations, and the same blocks keep appearing and reappearing; more repeating blocks than could ever be imagined.[8]

Coming out from the projects, onto the Bowery, from my odyssey among the browned blocks of Alphabet City and Stuyvesant Town – which could be likened to a plodding and lugubrious music with little in the way of either melody or harmony – my 'visual ear' was caught by an extreme case of raucous, and thrilling, urban jazz. The Bowery frontage – of which the New

The Bowery, East Village, New York
A family of vernacular buildings at differing scales: one song, many voices.

Museum (by architects SANAA, 2007) and the Sperone Westwater Gallery (by Foster + Partners, 2010) are a part – is unforgettable. Here we have buildings old and new, large and small; all similar but none the same; all singing one song, but in a lavish variety of ways. The majority of the blocks are traditional 19th- or 20th-century commercial tenement buildings. They have similar windows, cornices, ground-floor frontages and fire escapes. However, their sizes differ radically: small, medium, large, extra large. The exterior design of the New Museum picks up the street music with great style, playing along with all the individuality of its own sounds and syncopations but enriching rather than clashing with the rest of the band. This is an urban harmony which in its context is both wild and wonderful.

As well as representing one end of the scale of 'urban harmonics', which can range from the well-mannered and highly controlled cityscapes of Bath, Beirut or Paris to the almost total free-for-all of many of the streets of London or Doha, this portion of the Bowery also reminds us of the distinction between a building and an urban block. An urban block is by nature made up of several buildings which together make the 'street wall'. A small urban block is 60 by 60 metres (200 by 200 feet) and a large one is 120 by 120 metres (400 by 400 feet). If the buildings on the Bowery did not touch each other, they would not be able to work together. In this case, where the block is a composite (a jigsaw) of individual elements abutting each other, either by design, by statutory control or by economic and historical circumstance,

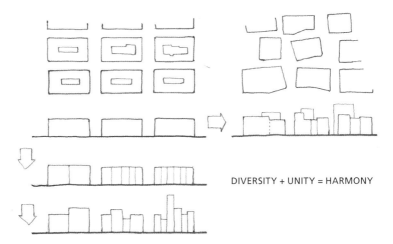

From out-of-scale to human scale: a process of rescaling and diversification.

DIVERSITY + UNITY = HARMONY

the block will take on more or less diversity of volume, facade proportion, material, building type and architectural language, but will to greater or lesser degrees cohere. If on the other hand one architect is asked to design a full urban block as a single building, he or she is faced with the challenge of achieving an appropriate scale and grain.

West 8, Borneo Sporenburg masterplan, Amsterdam, 2000
The masterly scaling of large and small components to achieve a living and eloquent grain.

One of the most thrilling examples of well-judged grain, both fine grain and the artful use of coarseness, is Borneo Sporenburg in Amsterdam, completed in 2000. The masterplan by West 8 is of a comparable size to Churchill Gardens; however, it is mostly low-rise, acclaimed as being the first high-density housing project in Holland to offer individual ground-level

access to the majority of units. Within the plan, which is made up of very diverse building types and architectures, the canal inlets (former docks) of Entrepothaven and Spoorwegbassin are notable.[9] They are lined with hundreds of one-off terraced houses, each of which is flamboyantly different from its neighbours in architecture and yet they are all almost identical in shape and size; the exact reverse of the Bowery. Far in the distance sits the 'Whale', a vast object-like apartment building, breaking the skyline in shocking contrast to the lower-lying housing around. If the townhouses are like fast-playing tunes and rich syncopations, from saxophones and trumpets, then the Whale in the distance is like deep chords coming from the bass, or a blast of trombones. It is good music.

The 'filigree' of the Borneo Sporenburg townhouses is distinctive partly because of the narrow frontage of each house. It is also quite out of the ordinary, in terms of the uniqueness of every single building. A balance has been struck between the 'oneness' of the group of buildings – their collective

The canal inlet of Entrepothaven at Borneo Island, Amsterdam
A balance of diversity and unity achieves a rich harmony.

scale is augmented by the fact that they speak a common language – and the plurality of their individual identities, breaking down the scale of the whole into a multitude of intimate conversations. This is a complexity which most developers cannot accommodate. However, whether it is considered an impossible dream, an artificial construct, a stage set of picturesqueness or simply an enlightened piece of 'slow urbanism', few visitors are not struck by its irresistible friendliness. It is a prime example of a humane attitude to urban design, even though it was developed on a very large scale and over a relatively short period of time. It is indeed helpful to us in seeking to redefine the words 'rational' and 'rigorous'.

Park Avenue, New York
A grand space for the city.

On Grain and Directionality

Returning to the analogy of wood grain – long grain and end grain
– directionality is another aspect of 'grain' in cities which should be
discussed. The long grain of Churchill Gardens is obvious. Long facades run
perpendicular to the river; their frame structures are inhabited with balconies,
walkways and bays. Like planks of wood, their narrow cut ends differ from
their broad linear faces. In typically systematic fashion, the end facades are
uniformly blank, even the ones facing the river. This is an imposed system,
which although it would have seemed entirely rational and rigorous, leads to
missed opportunities such as river views denied. Directional grain, however,
is traditionally a natural response to the organisation and orientation of
buildings and urban blocks, to context and climate.

It is surely natural that facades facing east or west should differ from those
facing north or south, or that a major frontage will differ from a minor one
in proportion, material and detail. If many urban blocks over a large area
of a city share common characteristics, for example the blocks of upper
Manhattan where larger buildings face wider avenues on the long grain and
smaller buildings (often townhouses) face the narrower streets on the end or

East 76th Street, New York
The Manhattan grid: larger
buildings face the wider
avenues; smaller buildings
face the more intimate cross-
streets.

cross grain, then the city as a whole is brought into a unity on a scale larger than any of its constituent parts. While reading the urban grain at the scale of its parts, of various correlated sizes, the city can also be read at the expanded scale of an entire neighbourhood. The Manhattan grid is so consistent across such a large area, meanwhile accommodating such immense diversity, and the difference between grains – avenues and cross-streets – is so great, that one could almost navigate the city blindfold, just by the differences in acoustic qualities created by the widths of the streets and the movement of cars. Zooming in on the details of buildings, if we find facades facing major streets in stone transforming to brick as we turn the corner onto a side street, or if windows are large and regular on the primary face and small and irregular on the return, then the scale of the street and the urban block is broken down to something finer, more complex or intimate.

It was the Commissioners' Plan for Manhattan of 1811 which set the grain of New York:[10] 100 foot [30 metres] for avenues – a great log cut into planks –

Wilton Crescent, Knightsbridge, London
Blocks can be articulated, and scales broken down, by facade treatments differing from one street to another.

60 foot [18 metres] for streets – sliced up into hefty chunks of timber, ready to be carved over time into a living city. At that time there was no clear-cut legislation on the size of plots or height of buildings to inhabit the grid, but it naturally emerged that larger buildings faced the larger, noisier thoroughfares and the smaller houses faced the quieter streets. Zoning was only introduced in 1916. There was also no aesthetic control imposed by the City, so people simply followed the norms of the time in terms of construction, proportion and materials, while also choosing ways of being as different as possible from neighbouring properties when they chose – like Borneo Sporenburg, but dictated by a free market rather than guidelines in a masterplan.

These are aspects of scale and grain in cities which can and will evolve over time, without any central control. However, masterplans and guidelines

Allies and Morrison, Porphyrios Associates and Townshend Landscape for Argent, King's Cross Central masterplan, London, 2007
The King's Cross Central masterplan for Argent displays linear grain which reflects the original 'railway grain' of the Goods Yard.

sometimes play an important part. The King's Cross masterplan for Argent by Porphyrios Associates, Allies and Morrison and Townshend Landscape (2007) is a good example of the conscious use of grain to shape a piece of a city, to give it coherence at the scale of the neighbourhood while connecting it to its context in time and place. The linear grain of the site from the days when it was densely covered by railway track, spreading like a river delta to meet the city, became a primary tenet of the masterplan guidelines.[11] The aim was to promote harmony or resonance between potentially disparate buildings – old and new, large and small. The long grain runs north–south, like the railway tracks and the historic goods yard buildings which followed them, and is now taking shape in the form of Google's UK headquarters, Cubitt Crescent and other blocks. The linear blocks are cut where they meet the sinuous line of the Regent's Canal and end grain is revealed.

At Msheireb in Doha, a city which from the earliest days was grained slightly off due north to catch the strongly directional prevailing wind, the streets are wider north to south and the blocks are longer; maximising wind and shade, the masterplan guidelines were set in this case to establish a prevailing grain and to differentiate between long-grain and end-grain facades, even to the point of giving different proportional guidance for quantities of glazing, relating to the optimum solar orientation of the various frontages. In this way a portion of the city is bound together by a common vernacular and so participates with the wider city in a set of scale-ratios which connect the individual building to the cluster (*fereej*), to the quarter, the neighbourhood and the city as a whole, each contributing to a sense of place and identity – locally, nationally and regionally.

History Speeded Up

The housing project at St Andrews, Bromley-by-Bow, developed by Barratt London in partnership with the London Development Agency and completed in 2013, pulls together many of these themes. Occupying a 3-hectare (7-acre) site by an above-ground section of London Underground's District line, just south of the Olympic Park, the masterplan, devised by Allies and Morrison, comprises three repeated longitudinal blocks containing nearly a thousand homes. Rather than being placed as freestanding rectangular boxes – like overscale packing cases, sitting side by side on a railway platform – each urban block is modelled to make the spaces between into carved 'outdoor rooms' and to set up what could be called a 'jazz dialogue'

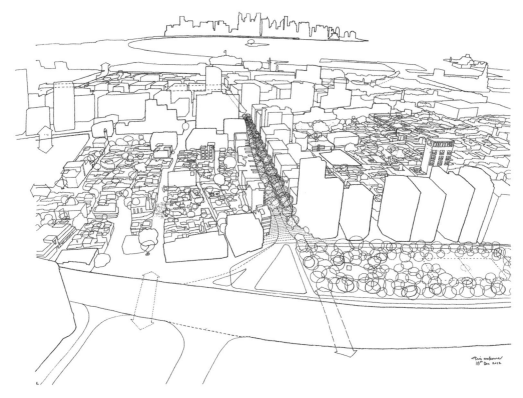

between facades. The urban blocks, which are similar to Churchill Gardens in length, are broken down into apartment buildings of a medium scale, wrapping around communal courtyards, each designed by different but like-minded architects: Allies and Morrison; Maccreanor Lavington; and Glenn Howells.[12] The individual buildings are all unique in subtle ways which reveal themselves as you examine more closely: the stripe of a brick wall; an offset balcony; a cutaway corner. Their folded facades and variegated skylines significantly reduce their apparent mass. There is rhythm among the group and syncopation too. There are repeating geometric lines; highs and lows create patterns, but from building to building around each block, and from block to block, the entire composition is enriched by numerous variations on a theme. The aim here, within the constraints of a fast-track programme, was to emulate 'slow urbanism': to achieve a scale-diversity which occurs naturally when urban blocks evolve organically over time, under different ownerships and with a variety of designs, but which needs to be contrived,

Makower Architects, aerial view of Asmakh and Msheireb, Doha, with West Bay in the distance 2012
Old Doha's grain from north to south, following the prevailing wind.

and guided by a masterplan, if all is to be delivered as a single piece, if human scale and fine grain are to be achieved. In Lynch's words quoted above, when development is fast, 'deliberate manipulation of the world for sensuous ends'[13] is required. It is important however to qualify Lynch's use of the word 'sensuous'. He is not referring to the exotic meaning of the word; rather he means the everyday world which we experience, with our eyes, noses and fingers, our minds and our emotions.

Allies and Morrison, Maccreanor Lavington and Glenn Howells for Barratt London, St Andrews Bromley-by-Bow housing development, 2013
Softened geometries and variety between facades are used to achieve human scale.

At St Andrews it was through the masterplan that a balance between unity and diversity was achieved, with each member of the band being encouraged to play along to the beat but in their own way, making a lively harmony. At the Bowery the jazz is held together not by a masterplan but by a binding vernacular; a consistency of building type, components and proportions; loosely unified but allowing for infinite variation. This is the lesson studied at St Andrews. The vernacular is literally a common language, allowing a consistent song to be sung in many voices. The decision of the developer, Barratt, to involve three architects working under a tightly defined masterplan, was enlightened. Even though the apartments were a 'mass-market product', and repetition to some degree was essential, to use a variety of architectural hands was a way of breaking down the scale of what could otherwise have been a monolith, like the World's End.

This is one of the fundamental 'control dials' in a masterplanner's toolkit: guidelines can be set for degrees of variation and interpreted by different architects in different ways. At one end of the scale, a free-for-all, with no consistency of building type, proportion, material or size, can result in

Bath, Somerset
All the buildings of Bath are built of the same stone, giving the entire city a sense of being like a harmonious choir.

cacophony. At the other end, too much control can produce a monotone. Meanwhile an appropriate level of urban harmony will differ greatly from one place to another, depending on context. The enlivening richness of east London could be out of place and destabilising in the genteel west-London district of Belgravia; conversely the delightful repetition of motifs and consistency of materials in the 18th-century neoclassical terraces and crescents of the English city of Bath, or more recently those of the public–private redevelopment company Solidere in downtown Beirut following the end of the Lebanese Civil War in 1990, could be too much for Borneo Sporenburg. It is a question of the relationships between buildings one to another and between groups of buildings and their wider context. The

Redevelopment by Solidere of broad street, Beirut
Degrees of consistency or variety in streetscapes around the world denote various characters and urban harmonies. Shown here is a recent remodelling of a historic Beirut street.

dynamic between the plural and the singular – between polyphony and monotony – is a question of urban scale. In Alain de Botton's words, 'when buildings talk, it is never with a single voice. Buildings are choirs rather than soloists; they possess a multiple nature from which arise opportunities for beautiful consonance as well as dissension and discord.'[14]

The dynamic between old and new is part of the grain of the city. Jane Jacobs asserts that 'cities need old buildings so badly it is probably impossible for vigorous streets and districts to grow without them'.[15] The collage of old with new, even when the new vastly outweighs the old, is like spice in a stew. To retain aged buildings may not be the simplest solution, nor the cheapest, but the richness which old things bring gives flavour to the urban experiences we feed off each day. Contrasts are enlivening and there is delight in the accidental, a thrill in the discordant or bizarre, in terms of scale as well as age. Whether it is a railway viaduct towering over cottages, or a sculpture in a public space, we are often pleased when we are surprised.

On Patina

This brings us to the third thesis of the book:[16] that we need to learn from old and undesigned things – from the cities, neighbourhoods and streets we love most, and even from Nature – to achieve patina. To quote John Summerson from *Georgian London*, 'A town, like a plant or an ant-hill, is a product of a collective, unconscious will and only to a very small extent of formulated intention.'[17] As designers, especially when developments are on a large scale and happening fast, we need to emulate that which is slow-grown and intimate. The masterplanner has a set of 'control dials' – geometry, volume, proportions, uniformity of layout, diversity of materials, numbers of designers involved, and to some extent building types and activities – but the one thing he or she rarely has control over is speed; that is the realm of developers and the marketplace. Urban grain, like the growing of a tree, develops over time and is essential to our experience and the character of cities. Are designers therefore obliged to think as non-designers sometimes, if they are to contribute to a city's humanity? Are they obliged to emulate nature and to celebrate the patina of time, especially when asked, as is so often the case, to do 'too much too fast'?[18] Patina is the quality of a surface as it develops naturally over time, but it can also be made by a conscious process of patination. Is the use of patination, at the scale of the city, which could be described as the 'urban picturesque', a falsifying or a humanising of the urban environment? Will it result in a loss of 'authenticity', or a fake film-set feel, or will it make a better place for people to inhabit? Opinions will differ, but the certainty proposed by this book is that the meaning of the word 'rational' – which can so often lead to an inhuman scale and coarse grain simply through an overreliance on the intellect – should be questioned, and furthermore that the importance of an active, intuitive and sensual connection between ourselves and our physical environment should be promoted by designers and non-designers alike.

References

1 Kevin Lynch, *The Image of the City*, MIT Press (Cambridge, MA and London), 1960, p 116.
2 John Summerson, *Georgian London*, Pleiades Books (London), 1945, p 9.
3 *Anonymous, 'The World's End Estate: Introduction and History', http://www.worlds-end.org.uk/files/Open_House_at_Worlds_End.pdf [accessed 4 April 2014]. An article published in the Architectural Review on the completion of World's End in 1977 described the estate as follows: 'If you put your architect's eyes in your pocket you see that you are standing in a sort of paraphrase of a medieval castle […] the internal courts have an air, not of modern domesticity, but of castle yards; while the squat galleries with their hard finishes, thick iron grilles and dark squalid corners, seem designed for the onslaught of brawling men-at-arms.' Quoted in James Dunnett, 'World's End, the pride of Eric Lyons', Building Design,* November 2008.
4 The author in conversation with a resident in May 2013.
5 *Westminster Conservation Area Mini-Guide 43,* May 2004, p 13.
6 Henry-Russell Hitchcock, 'Pimlico', *Architectural Review,* September 1953, pp 176–84.
7 Christopher Alexander, *The Timeless Way of Being,* Oxford University Press (New York), 1979, p 36.
8 Le Corbusier himself was a critic of the finer-grain aspects of the city which he found on his first visit there in the 1920s, contrasting them to his own visions: 'one is no longer confronted with the spires and campaniles of a wild Manhattan, jostling against one another and mutually robbing each other of light and air, but in majestic rhythm of vertical surfaces receding into the distance in a noble perspective and outlining pure forms.' *The City of To-morrow and its Planning [Urbanisme [1924], 8th edition, 1929],* translated by Frederick Etchells, Dover Publications (New York), 1987, p 282.
9 Mary Livingstone, 'Borneo Sporenburg Docklands', 2004, produced following Professor Jack Ahern's Landscape Architecture Study Tour from the Department of Landscape Architecture and Regional Planning at the University of Massachusetts: see http://courses.umass.edu/latour/Netherlands/livingstone/index.html [accessed 4 April 2014].
10 One of the driving reasons for allowing the Manhattan grid to carry straight along and across the island was to allow breezes to 'wash through' stale air. Remarks of the Commissioners for Laying out Streets and Roads in the City of New York, under the Act of April 3 1807, William Bridges, 1811.
11 King's Cross Central, Urban Design Statement and Guidelines, for Argent St George, London and Continental Railways and Excel,

2005, written by the author while director/partner in charge of the project for Allies and Morrison.

12 Allies and Morrison, where I was the partner in charge of the project, did the masterplan and the architecture of the first and last phases. The other two architects, Maccreanor Lavington and Glenn Howells, were chosen because their approach to design and aesthetics was similar to (but not exactly the same as) Allies and Morrison's.

13 Lynch, *The Image of the City*, p 116.

14 Alain de Botton, *The Architecture of Happiness,* Penguin Books (London), 2007, p 217.

15 Jane Jacobs, *The Death and Life of Great American Cities* [1961], Vintage Books (New York), 1992, Chapter 10 on 'The Need for Aged Buildings', Condition 3, pp 187 and 189: 'The district must mingle buildings that vary in age and condition, including a good proportion of old ones [...] By old buildings I do not mean museum pieces, not old buildings in an excellent or expensive state of rehabilitation – although these make fine ingredients – but also a good lot of plain, ordinary, low-value old buildings, including some rundown ones.'

16 For the first thesis of this book, regarding intermediary scale, see Chapter 1, p 33; for the second thesis of this book, regarding norms of scale, see Chapter 2, p 50.

17 Summerson, *Georgian London*, p 2.

18 John Rose, design director of Msheireb, as recorded by the author.

5

On Scale and Form

'He entered into a miniature world and right away images began to abound, then grow, then escape. Large issues from small … thanks to liberation from all obligations of dimensions, a liberation that is a special characteristic of the activity of the imagination.'

Dictionnaire de botanique chrétienne, 1851[1]

The city is made up of lumps of built material which come together to enclose space, inside and out. Each of these lumps, which sometimes touch one another, has both a footprint, its shape and size in the horizontal dimension, and a height in the vertical. If we walk from one end of a block to the other – be it an urban block or a building – without seeing a change, a break, or an opportunity to turn right or left, we ask whether it is over-scaled, or lacking in human scale; we may wonder where we are, or begin to feel lost; it may make us feel small. We perceive a building through our own movement; but even when standing still, our eyes travel its surface, gauging its scale and discerning distances and differences, even the slightest irregularity being something quite distinct from that which is entirely regular.

On Footprint

The Bank of England, Prince's Street, City of London, 2014
A large impenetrable urban block; a hindrance to movement.

To quote the Danish urbanist Jan Gehl, 'Homo sapiens is a linear, frontal, horizontally orientated, upright mammal'.[2] We are sensitive to horizontal distances, because this is how we move. The impact of verticals is less obvious since much of the time we look straight ahead, or even down at the ground. The footprint of a building the size of the Bank of England – the fortress of finance designed by Herbert Baker and completed in 1939, which replaced John Soane's masterpiece and was described by Nikolaus Pevsner as both 'oppressive and, worse, lacking in grandeur'[3] – may be too large to navigate with ease, in body or by eye. As members of the public we cannot walk through it, we have to find our way round it. We begin to think of it as an oversized object, perceived in fragments but experienced as a singular, potentially oppressive, monolith. As has been mentioned in Chapter 2, there are certain dimensional norms, related to the norms of human scale, which are significant in the making and experiencing of cities. These relate to the scale of buildings as much as they do to urban blocks and neighbourhoods. Our desire to be able to turn right or left, to permeate the urban fabric, after

Minoru Yamasaki, World Trade Center, New York, 1972
Soaring verticals and extreme height do not directly affect our experience of the city which is primarily a horizontal continuum, understood through movement.

walking a minute or two – between 50 and 70 metres (160 to 230 feet) – coincides with an engrained sense that a single building, in an urban context at least, of larger than those dimensions is in danger of being 'a lump' in the negative sense of the word: oppressive and inhibiting to movement.

Our reading of verticals however, such as the soaring mullions of the World Trade Center before 9/11, is not overpowered by sheer height in the same way. To walk between the Twin Towers in downtown Manhattan (by Minoru Yamasaki, 1972) – the 55-metre-square (180-foot-square) footprints of which are marked out today by the two vast voids of the National September 11 Memorial, clad in black stone and gushing unimaginable quantities of water – was to navigate urban forms of a familiar scale in plan, even though in elevation they were reaching to the sky and speaking to the scale of the city and beyond.[4] Height and breadth are relative but where breadth could be said to have natural limits of comfort, beyond which large pieces need to be broken down, the scaling of height is by nature more telescopic.

This chapter concerns scaling and shaping the physical form of buildings, in both horizontal and vertical dimensions. This is a function not only of physical encounters with buildings, by body and by eye, but also of intuitive readings and subliminal association, perceived by a metaphoric form of 'touch': close-up, as if with a microscope, or from far away through the lens of a telescope. Over time, parcels of land generally grow; buildings get bigger, and with the arrival of the elevator in 19th-century Chicago,[5] buildings began reaching unprecedented heights. In 19th-century London a gross floor area of four times footprint would not be uncommon, whereas in 20th-century Chicago or New York, this figure would rise to 10 or even 20 times. A natural balance is always found between height and footprint, between open land and density of occupation, governed largely by economics, the laws of supply and demand and of construction cost and technology, but fed also by ambition and to some extent greed.

If the normative unit of urban measure for an adult human being is the basic cell of the city, the house, then large buildings call for scale-ratios beyond the norm. This chapter is concerned more with bigness than with smallness and discusses not only the challenges of big scale but also its virtues and possibilities.

Responsive Form

We are in Doha again; it is 1952. The city is growing and the fine-grain filigree of the old town – a dense agglomeration of small, tightly packed houses and alleyways so narrow that even your children can reach from side to side with arms outstretched, and there is always shade, at least on one side or the other, except when the sun is at its highest – is increasingly being supplanted by broader, more spacious courtyard houses, because new-found oil wealth is flowing into the country at an ever-accelerating rate (see Chapter 3). A surveying plane manned by the Hunting Surveys aerial photography

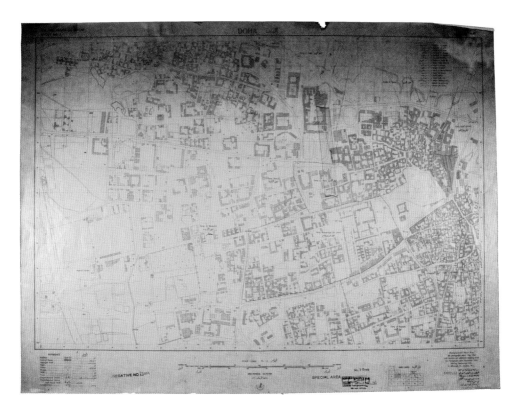

The Hunting Surveys plan of Doha, 1952
A detailed map, showing the soft informal patterns of Doha's early growth.

company[6] is flying overhead, taking high-resolution photographs of the city, while back at the Hunting HQ, draughtsmen are penning the definitive plan of the entire city: 22 sheets, now to be found at the British Library, so detailed that you can pick out each new house – the Al-Othman House where the first petrol pump was, or even the very room of the house where my friend's grandmother lived, just east of the Jalmood House, home of the slave trader who was named after the hardest rock in the desert.

Fast-forward to the large construction site in central Doha today – Msheireb – and four of those houses remain, encircled by large new structures, folded and fragmented in interesting ways. Three of the new buildings are nearing completion as this book goes to press: the Diwan Annex, the Amiri Guard and the National Archive, by Allies and Morrison, for which I was responsible.[7] As a group, they are 300 metres (1,000 feet) long – three or four minutes' walk from end to end – and together they form a still life: solid, sculpted

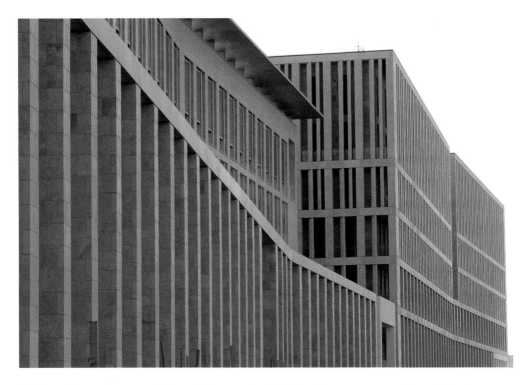

blocks, with carved spaces within and between. As a trio, they form a variegated frontage to the street, a family of three individuals. Of the three, the two end-stops, the Annex and the Archive, offer particularly useful examples of scaling form and surface.

Wind back a few years to 2008, when the brief for the Annex was being drafted by Msheireb Properties. It was to provide 50,000 square metres (500,000 square feet) of flexible office space; a rational and efficient container for work. As the early site assessments began, testing the irregular shapes of the site, narrowing and widening in accordance with eccentric landownerships and road patterns which long predated the Hunting Survey, a footprint of well over 100 by 100 metres (330 by 330 feet) was established for the Annex – enough to accommodate the required floor area while remaining respectfully lower than the Diwan, the impressive concrete palace at the crown of the hill, overlooking Doha Bay. The footprint was similar to the Bank of England, the impenetrable block at the heart of the City of London which interrupts an otherwise fine-grain street pattern. A rational plan for the Annex was drawn, with a single repeating grid spreading across the whole site, interspersed with regular lift cores and light wells. A sketch model was created and one began to imagine walking from one end of the building to the other: light well number one … light well number two … where am I? There is a difference between feeling lost in a building because the layout is complex and because it is so large and everything feels the same. In this case repetition was in danger of becoming disorientating; rational could become irrational.

Back to the drawing board and several sketches and conversations later, the building – still as large as the Bank of England – had been broken down into four parts. The parts share many characteristics in common, but each one is unique. The four 'building blocks' of the Diwan Annex, which is nearing completion as this book goes to press, are each organised with a regular plan, around its own rectangular courtyard. However, due to the irregular site shape – the unplanned lines of history etched into the land over generations – the four blocks are at four different angles. Where they meet, their facades are cut at surprising angles and between them a dynamic space, called the

Allies and Morrison, Diwan Annex, Msheireb, Doha, 2013
Four rectilinear blocks meet at various angles, stemming from the historical street pattern of Old Doha.

'Covered Street', becomes the heart or lungs of the building, with walkways connecting the four blocks, and bridges taking up the geometries.

From day one, the group of three buildings as a whole was called a 'family', and here in the Annex too was a family of forms: one family, four members – all individuals. The courtyards of each one were different – two indoors and two outdoors, some raised and some sunk deep into the basement and the facades, materials and detail from block to block differed in subtle ways – making it impossible to feel lost in a building which covers the same area as many hundreds of houses in the Doha of 1952.

Here again, in the making of a single building, we encounter the notion of 'intermediary scale', embracing both bigness and smallness, both the singular and the plural. The Annex is one building but it has some of the characteristics of four. In terms of its sculpted form, steps of scale mediate between large and small through sequential layers of grandeur and intimacy, like a house within a house. We 'navigate' the plan, the footprint, the size and the shape of buildings with our bodies, as we walk, and also with our

Allies and Morrison,
Qatar National Archive,
Msheireb, Doha, 2013
Large and small, new and
old: responsive geometry.

eyes. We discern differences both consciously and unconsciously. From every angle, within and without, the Annex and its neighbours are 'alive' with differences: always in motion, never static. Regular rhythms and even harmonies can be perceived, but before monotony sets in, they are broken by the scaling down of a single large block into a cluster of smaller forms or the fragmenting of a straight line into facets.

At the back of the Diwan Annex, there is a meandering *sikka* – meaning 'lane' in Arabic (plural: *sikkat*). It forms a tight fissure between two tall walls and runs along the back of the low-lying heritage houses – the slave trader's house, the oil company's house, the Radwani family's house – built from the 1920s onwards at the edge of the harbour-town, in a place where good wells for drinking water were found. Their forms are softly modelled with the ups and downs of stair towers and rooftop *majlis* rooms; they are grand houses built by rich families in the early days of Doha's growth. Each one is a cluster of forms, interwoven with walls and colonnades, in themselves combining the grandeur of a fine home with the intimacy of shallow rooms, tight passages and small courtyards. Ahead of us as we walk is the third in the family of new buildings: the National Archive of Qatar. Like the Annex, it is a study in fragmentation, the product of a responsive approach to geometry, allowing irregularities to grow out of the particular characteristics of the site and to find their own natural relationships with the surrounding context. Meanwhile it displays another important aspect of scaling architecture: the carving of solid form.

The National Archive is a building of national importance: holder of the State of Qatar's government records. Its location at the corner of the Msheireb site is chosen to be visible both from the Bay and from the souk, in dialogue with the new city and the old. It also enjoys an active dialogue with Doha's two other bay-side monuments, the Amiri Diwan and the Museum of Islamic Art. These are large forms which, with the Archive, make a trio, each one scaled to be seen from the Bay. Doha Bay is a lens for the city, making the city legible. One feels one can hold it in the palm of one's hand. Like a lens, it can both reduce and magnify. The presence of the Archive, seen through the lens, has the qualities of large and small scale in balance.

At the early stages of designing the Archive, in 2008–9, calculations were made to make sure it was sized both for present needs and future growth, to serve its purpose for generations to come. It is not a small building and its scale is in dramatic contrast with the heritage houses behind and the souk encircling the burial ground, to which the National Archive forms a backdrop.

Allies and Morrison,
Qatar National Archive,
Msheireb, Doha, 2013
Simple forms, scaled to
be seen from the 'lens'
of Doha Bay.

With an analysis of the complex functional requirements of the Archive – a strong and welcoming public face with reading rooms and exhibition spaces, a large and secure storage stack and a support wing for administration and conservation – came a natural diagram where the building was broken down into three parts, each one finding its comfortable position in the nuanced geometries of the site.

This building, in the most literal sense of the word, has grown out of a dialogue with its context both in space and time. Physically it mediates the scales of the old and new cities: its north pavilion holds the street, while its south wing steps down to enclose the Eid Prayer Ground, the seasonal mosque open to the sky, originally built to the west of the town, looking towards Mecca. The stack, held between the two, is lifted up on a grand colonnade, framing the diminutive modelled form of the Radwani House, one of the earliest houses of the area. It is the unit of the house which constitutes the basic cell of the city's composition. The 'scale-equivalence' between the Archive and the house, which is a piece of archive material in its own right, is the means by which their relationship becomes a friendship, rather than a conflict. Like Russian dolls, one opens up to reveal the next.

There is a temporal dialogue too. The National Archive picks up, echoes and reflects narratives and resonances from the neighbourhood, so much changed since 1952, in details which are both explicit and latent. For example, the north pavilion, at a glance a simple box, steps and folds at its base to form a point of interlocking with the stack, working in parallel at the scale of the city and the scale of the house. This is also part of making a 'scale connection' between the large and the small. The slow-grown, simple forms of the traditional buildings are elusive; they cannot be fully understood at a glance. On drawing closer they reveal the tracings of time. The new Archive does the same.

Grandeur and Intimacy

In our study of scale and form so far we have looked at large buildings: how, if carefully scaled, sheer size can sometimes be an enhancer rather than a detractor for a human environment; using intermediary scale to touch the middle point between large and small; offering grandeur for the child and intimacy for the giant; and encouraging each one to 'reach out and touch'.

Abdullah bin Saad House, Al Wakrah, 1940
A small building with a grand presence.

An equivalent process applies to small buildings, as is well illustrated by the traditional houses of Qatar. The Abdullah bin Saad House at Al Wakrah, built in 1940,[8] is a good example of a small house with a scale which is 'larger

than life', mainly on account of its double-storey *majlis* building which presides over the modest walled courtyard with extraordinary presence, enhanced by the seeming grandeur of the small but handsomely detailed external stair and the richly ornate adjacent *liwan* or portico. Whether aggrandising a small building or humanising a large one, it is through an intuitive understanding of scale-ratios that scale can be conjured into architectural magic.

No one was better at this magic art than Le Corbusier, master of architectural muscle, richness and restraint. It is interesting to compare the compact gallery wing of the Maison La Roche (1925), in the 16th arrondissement of Paris, now the Fondation Le Corbusier, with his vast 'container ship' of stacked dwellings, the Unité d'Habitation in Marseilles (1952). It is apparent on visiting Maison La Roche that it has a peculiar sense of scale. It is as if this were a house designed for a slightly larger site, which had to be shrunk at some point. It is broken down into

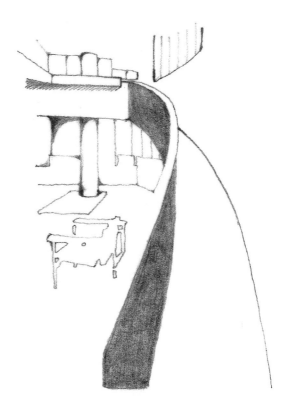

three parts and everything is slightly smaller than expected. But this is not disturbing; it is both intimate and imposing at the same time. Le Corbusier was not deterred by the tightness of the plan from accommodating his 'big ideas', such as the narrow ramp in the iconic gallery space or his bold use of coloured planes to add to the spatial flow of the house. The building is full and rich. To quote Robert Venturi's riposte to Mies van der Rohe, it is exemplary of the idea that 'more is not less'.[9]

The Unité d'Habitation, like a ship, is a singular object,[10] floating in a sea of green open space; but although one could argue that its immense form could have been broken down into smaller parts, there is something extraordinary and benign about its scale, on account of its gradation. The image of a hand inserting a single unit of habitation – one apartment – into the design model of the concrete frame is profound. It was created to explain the cellular concept of stacked and interlocking double-height, dual-aspect

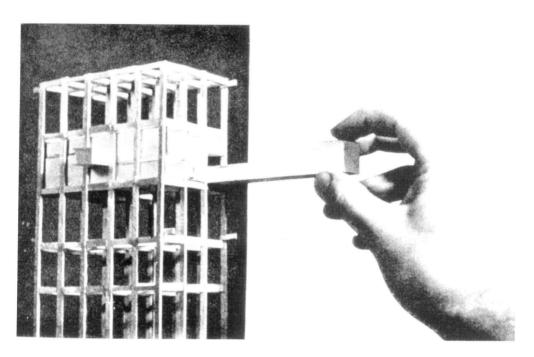

Le Corbusier, model for the Unité d'Habitation, Marseilles, 1950
Scaled to the unit of the family dwelling.

dwellings. The giant is 'touching' the cell structure of an inhabited 'beehive' of habitation, while the child is enjoying a cottage in the sky.

Lessons in scale from Marseilles can be seen in the tower by Allies and Morrison at St Andrews, Bromley-by-Bow (2013),[11] where the intent was to avoid creating a 'looming slab', looking out over the Lea Valley, at the high point of the site where the A12 crosses the London Underground's District line, and instead to create a building with a lively spirit and a friendly face. To achieve this, the block of 180 homes was disassembled back to its constituent parts. The footprint is a simple rectangle of 45 by 16 metres (150 by 52 feet), with nine units of varying size on each floor simply extruded from bottom to top. Ways of allowing the individual scale of each dwelling to be legible were explored: by breaking down the horizontal into the individual unit widths, meanwhile enhancing the vertical with deep recesses between the units. The result was a cluster of mini-towers, of various brick colours and a variety of heights.

At this point a brief interlude on the subject of building tall is appropriate. It is a subject on which several of the wisest visionaries of 20th-century urbanism

have suffered from hang-ups. To quote Jan Gehl: 'Above the fifth floor, offices and housing should logically be the province of the air-traffic authorities. At any rate, they no longer belong to the city';[12] or Christopher Alexander: 'There is abundant evidence to show that high buildings make people crazy.'[13] Perhaps they are overreacting to Le Corbusier's misguided insistence that vast open spaces should surround buildings of great height and persistent regularity; however, both of these luminaries are missing the point. Tall buildings are a valuable, if not an essential, part of good city making; it is simply a question of scale. The challenge, and the delight, is to achieve a good balance: between vertical and horizontal relationships; of space, form and surface; between unity and diversity; and between composition and detail.

Although not the tallest building in the world, the tower at St Andrews, Bromley-by-Bow aims to be, in the words of the American architect Louis Sullivan (dubbed 'the father of the skyscraper'), 'every inch a proud and

Allies and Morrison for Barratt London, tower for St Andrews, Bromley-by-Bow, London, 2013
Each unit within the plan is extruded to make a cluster of intermediate-scale forms.

soaring thing'.[14] It enjoys being tall. It jostles vertically upwards and makes protected places on the skyline, cutaway terraces, for the passer-by to inhabit by projection and for the resident to inhabit in the flesh. Tall buildings, whether modest as in this case, or immense as in the case of Manhattan's tallest structures, not only bring density and intensity to a city but give it body and shape. Viewed from outside, they can indeed loom, and diminish our experience at ground level, or they can magnify it. It is both a question of how they meet the sky and how they meet the ground; of how their surface is modelled and how they talk to their neighbours. From within, provided there is good access to green open space, a tall building can be a haven in the city; and so long as the elevators work well, it can enable city dwellers to feed off the best of city life and in turn to feed it with energy. To pick up Jan Gehl's point, they can be part of helping us feel that we belong in the city, and that it belongs to us.

In all the projects described above, we see a balance being struck between large scale (grand) and small scale (intimate), to make the best of both. It could be argued that this aim to achieve a 'middle point' of scale sounds like a desire to normalise, to avoid extremes; however, if on the one hand it is 'ordinary' to allow buildings to be what they want to be (and there is nothing wrong with ordinariness) – to design and construct them with walls, roofs, windows, doors, stairs, rooms, gardens, budgets and so on, to perform a function – then the focus of this chapter on the other hand is indeed to go beyond ordinariness.

The majority of the buildings we looked at along the Bowery in Chapter 4 are ordinary. In spite of their extreme differences in size – large, medium, small – they all share familiar archetypal characteristics: proportions and details relating back to the scale of the human body. However, together they amount to an extraordinary piece of cityscape, albeit entirely unselfconscious. A consciousness of the scaling of buildings in their urban context is helpful: the willingness to tune up the 'touch' of buildings as perceived from close up and far away – the jazz of a street frontage, the crank in a wall, the step in a parapet line, the thickness of a column; sometimes to simplify, sometimes to amplify, sometimes to enrich – these are basic steps in a good design process. If there is a narrative here, it is the narrative of the everyday but spoken with poetry as well as prose. If there is a reality, it is a reality enhanced.

The desire to celebrate norms of scale in architecture underlies the notion, discussed above, that it is good to 'break down' the scale of large buildings

by consciously employing intermediary scale. There are, however, many cases where architects have achieved great and surprising works by 'blowing up' the scale of something small to become something large – sometimes to extraordinary degrees. In this case the narrative is of the metaphoric rather than the everyday, involving a transformation from the real to the super-real.

'Urban jazz' frontage on the Bowery, Lower East Side, New York
The New Museum (2007), by architects SANAA, plays its part in the surprising harmony of the street.

Blow Up

As designers we rarely draw or model our thoughts at full scale. It is normal to miniaturise in order first to comprehend, then to communicate. We can shrink our subject in order to hold it in the palm of our hand or to guide it with the tip of our pencil. Or we can zoom in, getting closer and closer, and as we see less and less of the whole, we see more and more of its nature. It was Henry Moore, master of scale, who famously used miniatures, not simply to begin his explorations but to complete the final form of sculptures, working with clay between his fingers, to be blown up: 10, 20, 50 times. Looking closely at, touching and emulating natural objects such as the water-worn shapes of chalk-covered flints, Moore's work was characterised by the continual creation of scale-ratios: between the miniature, the normal and the super-scaled. In his own words, the sculptor 'gets the solid shape, as it were, inside his head – he thinks of it, whatever its size, as if he were holding it completely enclosed in the hollow of his hand.'[15]

Henry Moore's hands, 1976
The sculptor developed his works as hand-sized maquettes from which enlargements were then made.

I am holding a small piece of 'desert rose' in my hand. It has been sitting by my desk for many months. It was picked up in the desert outside Doha, and has

been forgotten since. On close examination, its interlocking forms fascinate, like flying saucers crashed together in a petrified state of collision; or perhaps they are emerging, preparing to take flight. Looking closer still, the individual grains of sand from which each flying saucer is made can be distinctly seen; I have never noticed this before in a piece of desert rose. Indeed these are particles from the actual sands of Qatar, held, as the *Oxford English Dictionary* explains, in 'rosette formations of gypsum crystal clusters, containing abundant included sand grains, the "petals" of which are flattened on the crystallographic axis, tending to occur in arid sandy conditions, such as the evaporation of a shallow salt basin'.[16] Looking from the desert rose – a crystal made of gypsum and sand – to the jewel-like pockets of gypsum crystal in the sample piece of Qatari limestone, prepared in 2011 for the National Archive project (another memento of the never-ending journey of exploration), I am reminded of the fact that gypsum is the material from which all the white render coatings and patterned plaster panels in Qatar were traditionally made; it is the colour of Qatar's architecture.

On arriving in Doha from the airport in 2014, one beholds, under construction, a massively enlarged desert rose: Jean Nouvel's design for the National Museum of Qatar, emerging from a forest of cranes; the coming together, crystal-fashion, of thousands of tonnes of steel and concrete. The National Museum is an extreme case of super-scale; both close up and from

Desert rose
A crystallisation of sand grains and gypsum.

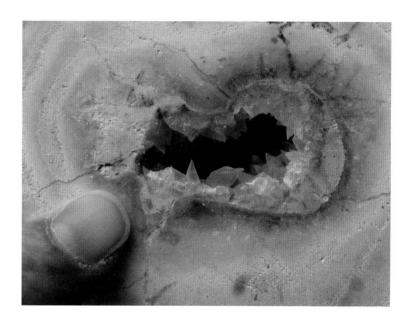

Qatari limestone
A pocket of gypsum –
the substance of Qatar.

far away. Its context, near the south end of the Corniche, is within a part of the old town where almost all the original buildings have been demolished now, except the old Amiri Palace. To say that the new building is 'out of scale' with its context is meaningless; it defies, and perhaps transcends, scale. It encircles the old palace, itself a cluster of tiny boxes, a crystallisation of traditional Arab urban form. Although it is as yet impossible to understand the exhilaration or shock of contrast between the gargantuan rock form of the new museum and the doll's-house palace, the half-finished form of the building is already portraying a sense of scalelessness. It will serve as a lens, which sometimes magnifies, sometimes distances its subject, and perhaps even turns things upside down, as it is moved closer to and further away from its subject.

The design is both a monument and a metaphor; but a metaphor of what? In an interview at the Doha Architecture Forum in May 2013,[17] Jean Nouvel said that the building was itself one of the main exhibits of the National Museum. The 'narrative' connection between the little stone – timeless product of Qatar's sand and gypsum – and the vast museum is emotive; however, this was not mentioned in Jean Nouvel's explanation. Rather, he described it in more general terms as a symbol of contemporary Qatar, and a sculptural setting for emotion.

The Museum of Islamic Art (IM Pei, 2007) and the Sheraton Hotel (William Pereira, 1982), Doha
Major landmarks for the city, brought closer to each other by the Bay. The Museum of Islamic Art is in the foreground, and the Sheraton Hotel beyond.

So do visitors feel diminished by confronting this extreme enlargement of a small stone, or does it make them feel 'larger than life'? Seen from afar, the child is rewarded. It can reach out to touch the stone as if it were in the palm of its hand. The child has become a giant. As one draws closer, like Alice in Wonderland, one shrinks; but experience – and perhaps emotion – is expanded. As one approaches the stone, its surface texture becomes apparent; a crystalline pattern of fractal shapes which bear no resemblance to the granules of sand on the surface of the rock in my hand. The museum is not after all a literal enlargement of the stone, and why should it be? It contains habitable space inside, which the rock does not. As one moves into the stone, passing through layers of glass carefully hidden in deep shadows – frames buried to avoid breaking the flow of light and space – one is in an imaginary cave.

The building is not finished at the time this book goes to press, so its experience must remain imaginary at this stage; but, although many critics will accuse Nouvel of 'gigantism' and of being 'too literal' in his use of the desert rose, it is clear that the building will be transformative of our experience of the city – more to the good than otherwise. In the words of the 1851 *Dictionnaire de botanique chrétienne* [Dictionary of Christian Botany], quoted by Gaston Bachelard in his *The Poetics of Space* (1957) and used as

Ateliers Jean Nouvel,
Qatar National Museum,
Doha, under construction
in January 2014
The sight of tiny steelworkers
piecing together the
world's largest desert rose
is arresting as one arrives in
Doha from the airport.

the opener to this chapter, it will be an experience where 'images abound, then grow, then escape … liberated from all obligations of dimensions'.[18]

The National Museum cannot, however, be treated as a paradigm for the scaling of buildings in cities in general. The 'scale-ratios' discussed in the earlier part of this chapter bind the city together – buildings to each other and people to buildings – with a binding plurality, in a way which brings cohesion and enhances people's environment and their experience of the city. The National Museum will be in absolute contrast to its surroundings, offering no scale-gauge for people to make such connections. It remains to be seen how its impact will affect the small buildings and the fine-grain, run-down old streets of Hitmi, one of Doha's last remaining historic neighbourhoods just nearby. Hopefully Hitmi will be allowed to enter into a positive dialogue with this giant of culture, enjoying the extreme jump in scale rather than being lost to demolition. What is certain is that the boldness of the new museum as an agent of transformation will work in a strong and positive way.

Two Big Domes

Not far from Doha, another extraordinary museum by Jean Nouvel is under
construction, also pushing the boundaries of scale: the Louvre Abu Dhabi.
In contrast to the Doha museum, which lies close to the heart of the old
city, the Louvre Abu Dhabi is located out on Saadiyat Island where the only
context is sand, sea and sky. Perhaps as a direct consequence of its lack
of urban context, the 'idiom' of the building – and its scale too – is that of
the traditional Arab city, rather than being of a magnified natural object.
However, like Doha, it uses super-scale to transform the visitor's experience,
from child to giant and from giant to child.

The Louvre Abu Dhabi is a project with some famously beautiful drawings.
The ground-floor plan resembles an old neighbourhood in an Arab town.
Small near-rectangular shapes cluster informally together, threaded through
by winding *sikkat*, overlapping the water's edge. Very faintly visible on this
plan is a large circle, nothing more than a tinted shadow. What the circle
represents is clear on looking at the roof plan: a vast shallow filigree dome
oversails the entire museum, casting shade and forming a man-made sky.

As with the Doha museum, extremes of scale are used to transform
everyday experience into something far from ordinary; but unlike the desert
rose, which could be described as intangible and surreal in its magnification,
the Abu Dhabi dome will be a building to 'touch', and touch closely, not
in spite of but because of the scale of its fine-grain fragmented plan and
its vast oversailing roof. Rather than making visitors feel like small creatures
in a blown-up world, Abu Dhabi will perhaps have some of the 'giant
intimacy' of the Pantheon in Rome. On entering Hadrian's second-century
masterpiece, one feels strangely close to its nobly coffered concrete dome,
despite the vastness of the space. How is this? Is it the shaft of light from

Ateliers Jean Nouvel and
Artefactory, rendering
for the Qatar National
Museum, Doha, 2010
One of the original images of
the design, framing views of
the Amiri Palace.

Ateliers Jean Nouvel,
Artefactory, TDIC, Louvre
Abu Dhabi, plans for
Louvre Abu Dhabi, 2008
The original plans for
the museum, now under
construction. A single huge
structure oversails and
gathers together multiple
smaller forms.

the central oculus, striking the coffers, moving slowly as the earth turns? Or
is it the simplicity and roughness, or the depth, of the coffers themselves?
By whatever means, there is a scale connection here – something for
architects to ponder and to emulate. It is a great example – albeit an
extreme one – of the use of intermediary scale.

We are ahead of ourselves. This chapter is about scale and form, but we find ourselves talking about internal space and surface. However, if we take a step back, we find that the connection between these themes – between the interior of the Pantheon, the super-scaled museums of Doha and Abu Dhabi and the sculpting of form to achieve balanced scale-ratios, mentioned earlier in the chapter – brings us to our fourth and final thesis: the notion of 'touch' which underpins this and the last two chapters of the book.

Ateliers Jean Nouvel, Artefactory, TDIC, Louvre Abu Dhabi, rendering for the Louvre Abu Dhabi, 2008
The oversailing vault – a man-made sky – brings super-scale to the experience of the museum.

On Drawing

Touch, in the terms of this book, is both actual and metaphoric, and it applies both to the designer and to the experiencer of architecture. On the part of the designer, when exploring ideas on paper, or on the computer, the hand is in command of lines and shapes which appear as we draw, with what

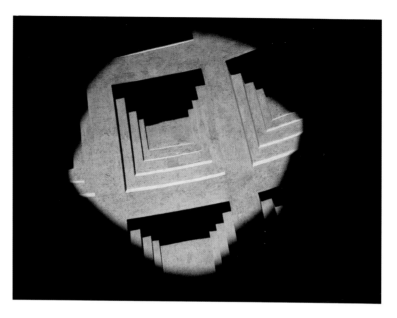

Pantheon, Rome, AD 125
The grand vault of coffered concrete.

sometimes feels like an almost electrical force. First they are not there, and then they are there. We can erase and alter them, extend and overlay them; we are in command. But they can guide us too. We do not necessarily know where they will lead us, and our eye (sister of the hand, as Le Corbusier suggested)[19] comments continually on what the hand has done. The Finnish modernist architect Alvar Aalto described his working process as follows:

> This is what I do – sometimes quite instinctively. I forget the whole maze of problems for a while, as soon as the feel of the assignment and the innumerable demands it involves have sunk into my subconscious. I then move on to a method of working that is very much like abstract art. I simply draw by instinct, not architectural syntheses, but what are sometimes quite childlike compositions, and in this way, on an abstract basis, the main idea gradually takes shape, a kind of universal substance that helps me to bring the numerous contradictory components into harmony.[20]

The process of drawing is a process of abstraction and is inherently miniaturised. We draw small, we imagine big. It is a process both of projection and empathy; imagining not just what we are drawing but our experience of what is being drawn. The pencil is the great connector between scales. From 1:2,000 scale to 1:2, we zoom out and zoom in

continually; but even when we zoom in, particularly if we hold a pencil rather than a mouse, we rarely draw at full scale. This is the metaphoric touch: imagined experience at a large and small scale simultaneously; eyes open, eyes closed; whether we are laying out a plan for a new city or shaping a moulding in stone.

The reliance on models created in three-dimensional computer space is taken for granted these days, and rightly so. Architecture and urbanism do not exist in two dimensions. But physical models are also an essential bridge between the emitter and the receiver of design. The British architect David Chipperfield, in a talk at the Museum of Islamic Art in Doha in June 2013, said that each one of his projects reaches a moment where a model at 1:30 scale becomes their essential tool; 'the first scale where one can really experience architecture'.[21] There are others who use much smaller scales to reveal and encapsulate the essence of a design idea. Like Henry Moore, the

Makower Architects, the process of drawing Zone 18, Doha, 2014
Showing the National Museum, an enlarged rock form, sitting among a repaired urban fabric of street and blocks.

miniature then forms a touchstone for the design process as it enlarges and moves into detail. Just as the sculptor likes to touch the materials of his or her work in the flesh, the designer or architect waits for the moment where we can touch a full-scale mock-up of crucial fragments of his or her idea. If time and circumstance are on our side, this will be an active part of the design process, rather than a bland process of signing off what was previously only captured in drawings and models; and now the designer overlaps with the experiencer of architecture.

In the flesh, and from the point of view of the users of buildings, touch is both physical – weathered wood at the tips of our fingers, worn brass in the palm of our hand, cold stone to sit on, glazed tiles to lean against – and it is metaphoric too. To touch with our eyes, to imagine buildings as small models, seen from far away, or to look into the surface of materials, seeing beneath their skin: this is the ability, and the delight, of going beyond touch. We are continually experiencing the physical world at our own scale and also at miniaturised and magnified scales at the same time. We began the chapter by talking about the process of navigating the shape and size of the buildings and blocks that surround us, from far away and from close up. This is how we read our physical environment and how we understand its scale in relation to ourselves: with our minds, our eyes and our bodies too.

Makower Architects, stone model of a mixed-use project in central Doha, 2012
Using large and medium-sized blocks to achieve intermediary scale.

References

1 This extract from a magical paragraph on the stachys byzantina as described in the *Dictionnaire de botanique chrétienne* [Dictionary of Christian Botany], 1851, is quoted by Gaston Bachelard in *The Poetics of Space* [*La Poétique de l'espace*, 1957], translated by Maria Jolas, Beacon Press (Boston, MA), 1969, p 154.
2 Jan Gehl, *Cities for People*, Island Press (Washington, DC; Covelo, CA; and London), 2010, p 33.
3 The building designed by Baker was described by Nikolaus Pevsner as the greatest architectural crime of the century in the City of London because of the demolition of John Soane's masterpiece which preceded it. Nikolaus Pevsner and Bridget Cherry, *The Buildings of England, London 1: The Cities of London and Westminster*, Penguin Books (Harmondsworth), 1957, p 183.
4 Yamasaki's World Trade Center (1972) provided 1.4 million square metres (13 million square feet) of office space and was 103 storeys tall. One of the towers would fit neatly into London's Golden Square.
5 The first tall building, made possible by Elisha Graves Otis's invention of the elevator in 1854, was Chicago's 42-metre-tall (138-foot) Home Insurance Building, opened in 1884. By 1888 the term 'skyscraper' had been coined.
6 Hunting Surveys Ltd, based in London, took high-resolution photographs of Doha every few years from 1948 to 1978. In 1952, they made a detailed plan of Doha and its surrounding land which was published in 1956. The survey was commissioned by the State of Qatar which was a British protectorate at the time.
7 'Phase 1a' is the first phase of Msheireb; three government buildings comprising 90,000 square metres (1 million square feet) of accommodation. The author was responsible for them from inception and has remained the guardian of their design through to completion. See also Chapter 2, note 20.
8 Ibrahim Mohamed Jaidah and Malika Bourennane, *The History of Qatari Architecture 1800–1950*, Skira (Milan), 2009, p 96.
9 Robert Venturi, *Complexity and Contradiction in Architecture*, MoMA, New York, 1966, p 16.
10 Colin Rowe and Fred Koetter, *Collage City*, MIT Press

(Cambridge, MA), 1978, p 68.
See also Chapter 3, note 14.
11 See Chapter 4, section
on 'History Speeded Up' and
note 12.
12 Gehl, *Cities for People*,
p 42.
13 Christopher Alexander, Sara
Ishikawa, Murray Silverstein,
Max Jacobson, Ingrid Fiksdahl-
King and Shlomo Angel, *A
Pattern Language: Towns,
Buildings, Construction*, Oxford
University Press (New York),
1977, p 115.
14 Louis Sullivan, 'The Tall
Office Building Artistically
Considered', 1896, quoted
in Alain de Botton, *The
Architecture of Happiness*,
Penguin Books (London), 2007,
p 217. Le Corbusier is also
quoted on p 242 of de Botton's
book as telling the *Herald
Tribune* on his first visit to New
York, 'Your skyscrapers are
too small.'
15 Henry Moore, 'The sculptor
speaks', in Philip James (ed),
Henry Moore on Sculpture,
MacDonald (London), 1966,
pp 62–4; quoted in Juhani
Pallasmaa, *The Thinking Hand*,
John Wiley & Sons (Chichester),
2009, p 18.
16 *Compact Oxford English
Dictionary*, 2nd edition, Oxford
University Press (Oxford), 1992,
definition of 'desert rose'.
17 Jean Nouvel speaking at
Doha Architecture Forum in
May 2013, as recorded by the
author.
18 See note 1.
19 'A hospital is a house of
man, just as the dwelling is
a "house of man". The key
being man: his stature (height),
his stride (extension), his eye
(viewpoint), his hand, sister
of the eye. His entire physical
nature is tied up in it, in total
contact with it.' Letter from Le
Corbusier to Carlo Ottolenghi,
11 March 1964, quoted in
Marida Talamona, 'Venice: a
lesson on the human scale',
in Jean-Louis Cohen (ed), *Le
Corbusier: An Atlas of Modern
Landscapes*, Museum of
Modern Art (New York), 2013,
p 135.
20 Alvar Aalto, 'Trout and the
mountain stream', in Göran
Schildt (ed), *Alvar Aalto In His
Own Words*, Otava Publishing
Company (Helsinki), 1997, p
108, quoted in Pallasmaa, *The
Thinking Hand*, p 73.
21 David Chipperfield speaking
at Doha Architecture Forum in
June 2013, as recorded by the
author.

6 On Scale, Skeletons and Surface

'... to explain a building, the upper story of which was erected in the nineteenth century; the ground floor dates from the sixteenth century, and a careful examination of the masonry discloses the fact that it was reconstructed from a dwelling tower of the eleventh century. In the cellar we discover Roman foundation walls, and under the cellar a filled-in cave, in the floor of which stone tools are found and remnants of glacial fauna in the layers below.'

CG Jung, 'Mind and the Earth', *Contributions to Analytical Psychology*, 1927[1]

When walking through Kew Gardens in west London, among countless magnificent trees, with beautiful shapes, leaves, colours and smells, it is difficult not to be struck by the Stone Pine;[2] why? It not only has a wonderful bone structure but you can also read the surface of its bark from a distance. It draws you towards it, revealing more as you approach. It has a 'tangible' texture from a distance and on getting closer, there are textures within textures. It is irresistible to touch when close but one feels one can touch it even from a distance; not only its finely balanced limbs but its surface also. This is intermediary scale at its best.

The Stone Pine, Kew Gardens, London
The scale and texture of its bark can be read at a distance. This is intermediary scale.

The Stone Pine, Kew Gardens, London
On drawing closer, the surface reveals richness and depth.

A different encounter is to be found at Rotten Row in Kensington Gardens where two super-scaled objects are to be seen on the horizon far away – the Shard (by Renzo Piano, 2013) and the Millennium Wheel (by Marks Barfield, 1999). Both feel like toys that can be touched and even picked up. They are out of scale with their context but in a good way. Moving on, by foot or by bike, they very soon disappear. Several miles through the city they reappear

Renzo Piano's Shard (2013) and Marks Barfield's Millennium Wheel (1999), seen from Rotten Row in Hyde Park, London
One feels able to pick them up from a distance. They then disappear from view; one can almost feel the curvature of the Earth.

again: closer and larger; larger than life. Of the two, it is the Shard which deserves consideration in the context of this chapter; it is the antithesis of the Stone Pine. One might admire it, and even delight in its shape and the extreme scale contrasts between it and its context, but the sheer featureless skin of each of its 'shard-like' planes has overwhelmed its other characteristics, to the point where, as with many of Renzo Piano's designs, it peels away from the bone structure for no apparent reason other than rhetoric. It is skin and bones but in denial of the bones.

Skin and Bones

There is no patina in the Shard. As discussed in Chapter 4, patina at an urban scale is part of the richness, intensity and complexity which we find in living cities. It is essential to the surfaces of buildings too: the plane of interface and overlap between public and private worlds. Patina connects buildings to their surroundings, through scale connections – large to small, near to far – and also through the dimension of time: depth and weathering.

Renzo Piano, the Shard, London Bridge, 2013
The smooth glassy skin makes the building feel scaleless.

Not far down the road from the Shard is Bankside 1/2/3, a development by Land Securities and IPC completed in 2007, for which I was the project

158

director and then partner at Allies and Morrison. Forming a group with the nearby former power station that is now Tate Modern art gallery (remodelled by Herzog & de Meuron, 2000) and the NEO apartment block (by Rogers Stirk Harbour + Partners, 2012), in an area that has never been subject to a masterplan, it is a cluster of three large office buildings, with shops at ground level and public spaces between. The largest of the three buildings – the Blue Fin Building (2007) – has been 'patinated' with randomly distributed, angled fins, not only to shade its glassy skin but also to bring its surface to life in depth and shadow as the sun moves through the day. The fins are held between horizontal ribs; the bone structure of the building comes to the surface. Blue Fin is a large office building, 12 floors in all. It cuts away at the upper levels and its base is eroded with pleasing complexity, like pebbles in a stream. However, its main planes are simple. It is an abstract backdrop to the street – a strong frame to Tate Modern on arriving from the south – but its surface is ambient, not encumbered by busy motifs and compositions.

The National Archive of Qatar, also by Allies and Morrison and mentioned in Chapter 5, is another case of a patinated surface, tuned to respond to

Allies and Morrison for Land Securities and IPC, the Blue Fin Building, Bankside, London, 2007
The facade achieves a rich 'patina' of shadow and light.

Allies and Morrison for
Land Securities and IPC,
the Blue Fin Building,
London, 2007
The west facade is an
abstract backdrop, a surface
alive throughout the day.
Seen from the Thames
foreshore at Tate Modern.

sunlight and connect to context. Its large facades are banded – like the
archive stacks within. Between the bands, 'super-slabs' are held; each one
a storey height and width. Each super-slab is made up of stones – stones
within stones – stacked like archive boxes on shelves. The stones are all from
Oman but from three different quarries, like cousins, and their skin tones
differ slightly. They are randomly distributed, creating a lively surface which
draws you in from a distance to come closer. The patina changes dramatically
through the day; it softens at dusk, a similar effect to the velvet-like stone
gable wall of Le Corbusier's United Nations Building in New York (1952).
The skin of the Archive is also carved in depth, inwards and outwards. Deep
reveals face south, cut with angled planes; projecting cills facing north and
east catch the sun coming round to create bright dots of light, even when
the facade is in shade, casting long shadows like a sundial as the sun moves
on. This building has both scale and patina, like the Stone Pine. Its surface is
active. But it also has muscle; it is not too fine.

In the north wall of the Archive, one of the large 'winking eye' windows contains the Sand Clock: a glass vessel, filled with sand from the desert, which rotates every hour to mark out the day. Looking through that window, across the 'lens' of Doha Bay at the towers opposite, there is one which stands out: the Burj Doha, by Jean Nouvel (2012). From a distance, its surface is smooth but with a lustre which draws the eye. As one approaches, the building's skin reveals itself to be made up of three layers: a single geometric pattern cut from silver metal plate, each layer of a different scale to the others. Behind the skin is a cavity, providing space for the window cleaners to do their work in safety. It creates a veil of protection from the harsh sun and filters the light within into a pattern of continually moving dappled shapes. This building is a beautiful object, sitting among the other isolated towers of West Bay; however, the profound thrill is in its skeleton.

On going inside, on being lifted – weightless – within the elevator shaft in behind the 'diagrid' structure, and on coming out onto an office floor,

Ateliers Jean Nouvel for His Excellency Sheikh Saud al Thani, Burj Doha, 2012
Clad in a richly patterned screen to shade its glazed skin, the building within is a mighty 'diagrid' skeleton of smooth concrete.

the benign immensity of the angled concrete columns is striking. They are irresistible to touch, smooth like an eggshell. From far away and close up, from outside and in, to explore this building is a continuous graded experience. This is not a building evolved and adapted over centuries, like Jung's house, yet it is indeed a building of layers, each of which reveals something new but, in Christopher Alexander's words at the start of the book, is 'supported by other patterns'.[3] To be inside the building is strangely like being inside a giant: the sense is of expansion, not diminishment. It enables us to understand what is behind the skin.

The skin of a building, even when it is shaped like a space rocket with no obvious ability to 'carve' adjoining public space, is also a skin to the air outside.[4] It is the plane of resistance and exchange between inner and outer worlds. And as we zoom out we are reminded that the continuum does not of course stop once we reach the edge of a building, it runs through the body and bone structure of the city. The surface of the city – pavements, shopfronts, facades, rooftops – is indeed supported by its spaces – streets and alleyways, squares and courtyards, parks and gardens; these are its vessels, organs, muscle and bones; a hierarchy of parts, a layering of interconnected scales. We remember Francesco di Giorgio Martini: 'the streets are the veins'.[5]

The Unité d'Habitation

The Unité d'Habitation in Marseilles (1952), described by Le Corbusier as 'the perfect receptacle for the family',[6] is also like the Stone Pine. Seen from afar, although huge, most people would agree that it has muscle, scale and depth. In the words of its maker, 'This immense building, 140 metres [460 feet] long and 70 metres [230 feet] high, appears familiar and intimate. From top to bottom, both inside and out, it is to the human scale.'[7] Although it is easy to disagree with Le Corbusier in terms of its form, in terms of surface, and its underlying bone structure, his bold statement is convincing. The building is a stack of containers, each container reading clearly within the whole. One can feel the fragile model of cardboard and balsawood, held in the architect's hand, enlarged to the scale of the family home, built of muscular concrete but fitted out with friendly colours and charming timber detail; it calls out to be touched, both close up and from a distance (please see page 139).

Le Corbusier, Unité d'Habitation, Marseilles, 1952
A typical apartment, scaled from the 'grand order' of the double-height space to the fine details of fitted seats and cupboard handles.

On arriving at the great cast forms of the ground-floor pilotis, it is time to touch again. This time it is the imprint of rough boarded concrete moulds and coarse timber grain embossed in the surface which draws the hand. It is the patina of this grand building: Le Corbusier's *béton brut*, inherited from his mentor Auguste Perret;[8] the scale of the giant, appealing to the child; softness found in the solid. The concrete of the Unité is the meeting of process and product, and again, the dimension of time is captured in built form.

On walking into an apartment from the inner chamber of the central corridor, the narrow linearity of the dwelling – only 3.66 metres (12 feet) wide – is noticeable; all dimensions have been tuned. The sense of contraction within – the hallway ceiling is only 2.26 metres (7 feet 5 inches) high – in contrast to the vast expansion of the glazed double-height spaces where they meet the facades, with strongly modelled balconies and sliding folding doors, further opening up relationships to air and light, is memorable. The sense of the ordinary tuned-up to the extraordinary, and the tangible feeling of interconnected scales, in each case substantial and robust, which grades this massive building down to the scale of the window seat with a unified set of elements, is remarkable. On reaching the roof, we find a world within a world, in turn cradled by the rugged arms of the surrounding mountains. It is a children's playground, surrounded by high walls; a microcosm of the city in its setting. This still life of sculpted forms includes two miniature mountains,

Sketch (2014) by the author after Le Corbusier, Unité d'Habitation rooftop, Marseilles, 1952
The rooftop is a microcosm of the community, a place for children and families.

sculpted by a Sardinian mason, Salvatore Bertocchi,[9] in hand-smoothed concrete, with small pockets for plants to grow. Significantly one of the play-hills is photographed in Le Corbusier's published works, set against the pure horizontal of the high parapet, in dialogue with the craggy skyline beyond.

Le Modulor

Unusually for a piece of writing on the Unité d'Habitation, we have reached the roof without yet mentioning the system of the Modulor. Le Corbusier described his dimensional system, of which the Unité is one of the most significant examples, as 'A harmonic measure to the human scale, universally applicable to architecture and mechanics'.[10] In 1946, Professor Einstein wrote to Le Corbusier about the Modulor, after their meeting in Princeton, as follows: 'It is a range of dimensions which makes the bad difficult and the good easy.'[11] As with so much of Le Corbusier's work there is a political layer, as well as layers of philosophy, aesthetics and technology. The Modulor emerged from a realisation – unresolved to this day – that America's (and in those days Britain's) system of measure, which has the beauty of linking all scales back to the human anatomy – the foot and thumb (the inch) – is incompatible with the European measure of the metre, the latter being derived from the circumference of the Earth, as opposed to the human body.[12] Thinking big as always, Le Corbusier saw a need for a universal harmony: something that not only can bind continents and world industries together, but also can connect the height and length of a whole building to the dimensions of an apartment, a room, a kitchen worktop or a door handle.

In his 1928 lecture 'Une maison – un palais' [A House – A Palace], Le Corbusier quoted the French nobleman and military officer Jacques de la Palice (or la Palisse) (1470–1525) as saying: 'the eye can only measure what it can see. It does not see chaos, or rather it sees things badly in a chaotic or muddled environment.'[13] The notion of visible order (as opposed to chaos) being the discernible manifestation of a latent harmony, founded in geometry and linked back to the human body, is worked through over and over again in Le Corbusier's early work. So what is this order? Is it an indefinable and subjective idea of beauty; something which some people will find pleasing and others will not? And what has it to do with surface? The illustration of Michelangelo's 1546 design for the Piazza del Campidoglio in Rome that appears in Le Corbusier's book *Vers une Architecture* [Towards a New Architecture] (1923) is telling. It is overlaid with six diagonal lines making three

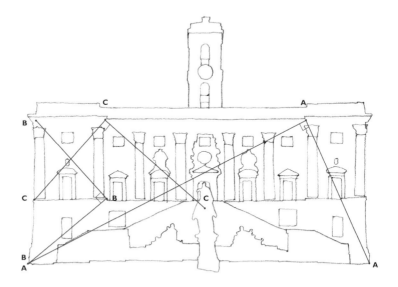

Sketch (2014) by
the author after Le
Corbusier's 1923 analysis
of 'regulating lines' at the
Piazza del Campidoglio,
Rome
The recurrence of
proportions from small to
medium to large creates a
'resonance'.

right angles of different scales, connecting different parts of the facade and
relating them to each other. These, in Le Corbusier's terms, are 'regulating
lines' and they provide evidence, in the context of the Fibonacci series and
the Golden Section, that there are powerful harmonies to which we all
have access and through which we all participate in an ancient proportional
tradition.[14] In terms of the passer-by, we can argue that it is the recurrence of
similar things at different scales, like the three right angles, which establishes
harmonious scale-ratios – commonly known as 'proportion', even if in many
cases this is only unconsciously perceived.

Geometry and Proportion

This brings us back to the subject of surface: how its composition, texture
or patina makes connections between scales, not only in the plane of the
skin but also in depth, into the body. The Unité d'Habitation is a set piece
of the conscious use of regulating lines. Its own outline is a proportion of
1:2½ which recurs in the overall facade, the intermediary 'super-bay' and
the horizontal panels of the dwellings, and is used in combination with
the double-height square opening to mark out the proportion and scale of
the individual homes, stacked one upon another to create the whole. We

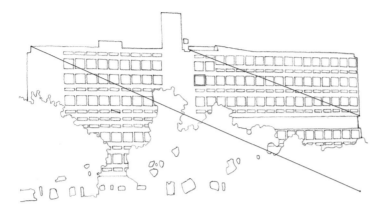

Sketch (2014) by the author looking at recurring proportions, found at various scales, in the facades of Le Corbusier's Unité d'Habitation, Marseilles (1952)
Le Corbusier applying lessons from the classics.

arrive again at the aedicules of John Summerson: the elements of a building which come together to make a building, each of which has something of a miniature building about it.[15] However, while we enjoy abstractions, and like to intellectualise, the reassuring thing about the Unité is that its source, its root, is the actuality, rather than the abstraction, of connecting to the human body and touch of man, woman or child.

The Modulor is in the grand tradition of classical proportional theory. From Vitruvius in the first century BC to Leon Battista Alberti, Leonardo da Vinci, Fra Giocondo, Francesco di Giorgio Martini, Sebastiano Serlio and Andrea Palladio in the 15th and 16th centuries AD, the human body is seen as a key to beauty, something to unlock magic secrets with which we hone and validate architecture. Rudolf Wittkower quotes Vitruvius describing how a well-built man fits with extended hands and feet exactly into the perfect geometrical figures of the circle and square: 'This simple picture seemed to reveal a deep and fundamental truth about man and the world, and its importance for renaissance architects can hardly be overestimated.'[16] Alberti summed up the connection between mankind and Nature, and between beauty and architecture, in the word *concinnitas*: 'Beauty is a form of sympathy and consonance between the parts within a body, according to definite number, outline, and position, as dictated by *concinnitas*, the absolute and fundamental rule in Nature. This is the main object of the art of building, and the source of her dignity, charm, authority, and worth.'[17] These theories seem to speak more about the abstraction of number and geometry than the actuality of physical experience, but this is where the intangible and the tangible meet.

Sketch (2014) by
the author after Le
Corbusier's Modulor
(1943)
An exploration of the
connectedness of scales.

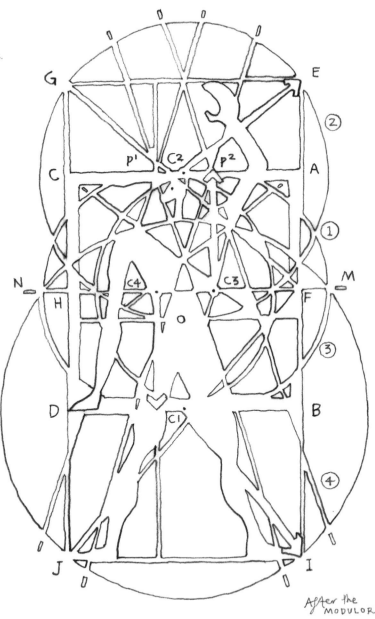

After the MODULOR

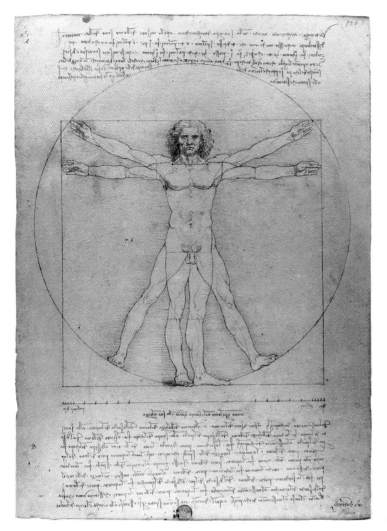

Leonardo da Vinci,
Vitruvian Man, c 1485
Proportional analysis of the
human body as a basic unit
of architecture.

The notion of proportional relationships being a key to beauty, not simply
in the plane of a facade but throughout the city, from head to toe, is
exquisitely illustrated in Alberti's seminal Palazzo Rucellai, completed in
Florence in 1451. The Palace itself has many stories to tell: how it is carved
into (or out of) a complex and ancient urban block on a narrow street;
how asymmetries are balanced inside and out to achieve a responsive and
harmonious order; the Renaissance art of 'imperfectionism' is at work. It is

on the other side of Via della Vigna Nuova, however, that we can understand how an idea of proportion permeates beyond the confines of the house, and blurs the boundaries of the home. With two simple interventions, the palace is magnified in range and depth, 'scaled up' to meet the city. Firstly, the diagonal block opposite has been cut away, to create a small triangular piazza, forming a perspectival space which literally makes the main facade seem larger than it is, as if through a lens. Secondly, one of the flanking facades on the square is carved to form a public loggia: a place where Giovanni Rucellai would meet friends and neighbours, in a realm both public and private at the same time.[18] Here we see how the question of scale and surface is inextricably bound to the skeleton, not simply at the scale of individual buildings but at the scale of the city.

The Grand Order

Returning to the Stone Pine, what is unusual about its bark? It is broken down into substantial pieces: large units with deep-cut veins between. Each of these is made up of many smaller flakes and fragments, like the bark of most trees, which can be seen at close range but from a distance merge into a surface texture. As with so much of Nature, from cow parsley to coral, the tree has a 'grand order': the recurrence of scales within scales.

The 'large unit' of the Unité is the duplex apartment, revealing its bone structure and giving intermediary scale, equivalent to the bark-pieces of the pine. It brings the building closer to touch visually, as seen from a distance. Within the grand order its windows become part of a texture at the scale of the individual, where the two-storey unit is at the scale of the family. The building was conceived as an entire community, ordered by scales within scales: community, family, individual, cat. Does the grand order make the building feel smaller or does it bring it closer for the eye to touch?

In the classical tradition it is common enough to find more than one storey combined into a single 'grand order', in one sense to bridge scales between the large (building) and the small (person) – to humanise – and in another to exaggerate the giant scale, often for reasons of political or social hierarchy. There is no more eminent example of the use of the grand order than Michelangelo's Piazza del Campidoglio.[19] The three buildings surrounding the iconic piazza at the top of the Capitoline Hill are not large buildings like the Unité, but in this case Michelangelo's motive for using the grand order –

Cow parsley
The 'grand order' is found in Nature as well as in architecture.

columns of double height, combining the first and second storeys together, which Summerson called the 'colossal order'[20] – was to aggrandise, not only the buildings but also the experience of the viewer; to add a giant-like dimension to the 'outdoor room' of the piazza, bridging between the scale of the individual and the scale of the city below. The 'larger than life' effect is also due to the enhanced perspective of the palaces on either side which splay apart, making the Palazzo del Senatore in the middle seem larger, or closer, than it actually is. It is interesting to observe how the sculptures mounted on the balustrade at the top of the palazzi seem 'too small', on account of being life-sized rather than enlarged.

In current developments around the world, as buildings grow larger and larger, often suffering from an unintended sense of scalelessness, there is a place for the grand order – sometimes used to great effect and sometimes less so. Eric Parry's handsome office building in the City of London, 5 Aldermanbury Square (2007), is a good example. By the division of its 20 floors into 10 'grand storeys', combined with the pleasing use of entasis as the volume reduces very slightly towards the top, the building in one sense appears smaller and in another 'grander' than it is. One could argue that there is no logic for the grand order based on the bones of the building; every office floor is the same; this is not the Unité where the double storey directly relates to the layout of apartments. However, it is successful; a scale-ratio has been established between the building, the person on the street and the surrounding context. A charming dialogue is also at work between Aldermanbury Square and its fine neighbour – Wood Street Police Station (by McMorran & Whitby, 1966) – which as well as entasis of the quietest and most minimal kind, simply uses a string course every other floor to mark out a grand order within its regular array of arched windows.

The grand order can be used as a mere visual trick, to make buildings seem smaller than they are. Perhaps this is the developer's dream, a way of achieving more gross area by stealth. However, this is intermediary scale at work – rescaling the city – and should not be dismissed as superficial or subversive. It is interesting to imagine a city where a universal guideline was set dictating that grand orders should be used on all main streets. It would be off-putting to some architects, those who worry that if the intrinsic order

Michelangelo, Piazza del Campidoglio, Rome, 1546
The grand order of the facades serves to make the space of the piazza both grand and intimate at the same time.

of a building – its skeleton – is not faithfully expressed on the exterior, it will be in some way dishonest. Scale is the perception of size, as experienced by human beings, and a street with a grand order will always be different from one without. Opinions will differ as to how use of the grand orders affects our experience of the city. Suffice it to say, however, that it is of value, both for the conscious manipulation of scale by designers and for the often unconscious responses of the person on the street.

Micro-Order

There are several notable examples of a 'micro-order', rather than a grand order, being used to manipulate the scale of buildings as perceived externally, and also from within. At Education City in Doha – a university campus rejoicing in an extraordinary collection of super-scale iconic structures – the headquarters of Qatar Foundation, by international architecture practice OMA, is nearing completion as this book goes to press. For each of its 14 floors, there are three tiers of 'miniature' openings, making a screen of modestly scaled square windows – a surface which pulsates as the ratio of solid to void softly adjusts in relation to the dramatically eroded spaces of the interior. The building is a simple box, sliced at the eighth floor, and its surface in one sense defies normative scale. It is impossible to know how many floors are in the building, or to

Eric Parry, 5 Aldermanbury Square, London, 2007
Eric Parry's building is seen at the centre of the photograph, with Wood Street Police Station by McMorran & Whitby (1966) in the foreground. Both buildings use the grand order.

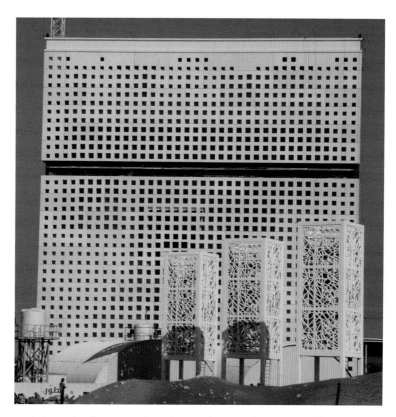

OMA: Qatar Foundation
Headquarters at
Education City, Doha,
2014
Micro-order in action: the
facade as surface.

read the scale of a person from its exterior at a glance. Its windows are like the bark-pieces of the pine tree but in a very different way from the Unité. In another sense, however, the design strangely reflects the modest scale of traditional Qatari buildings where facades are commonly broken down into smaller units, of two or sometimes three per floor.

The common theme within this chapter is that surface is the connector between the inner world of buildings – not just their skeleton but their heartbeat and bloodstream too – and the city. Buildings have skin and bones; so do cities. Surface is the shell which encloses space – interior or exterior. It is what connects the scale of the individual with the scale of his or her built environment. Buildings are large things made up of smaller things: floors, windows, balustrades and so on. Their scale-ratios can be tuned, firstly to achieve comfort and secondly to reveal something extraordinary, latent within the ordinary. If we revisit the four theses of this book – intermediary scale;

the child and the giant; patina; and touch[21] – all these are borne out in the making of surfaces, sometimes known as 'designing the external envelope'. Architecture and urban design are not dissimilar from alchemy: they are a process of transformation, from raw material to something of greater value – hopefully something of music and magic – to be felt by us all either consciously or unconsciously.

References

1 CG Jung, 'Mind and the Earth' [part of 'Die Erdbedingtheit der Psyche', 1927], *Contributions to Analytical Psychology*, 1927, Read Books (London), 2008.
2 Stone Pine, *Pinus pinea*, is native to Southern Europe. It is the source of edible pine nuts.
3 See Introduction, opening quotation and note 1.
4 'Around the living being, or rather through it and by means of the filtering action of its surface, there is affected a continual circulation from the outside to the inside, and from the inside to the outside, constantly maintained and yet fixed within certain limits.' Michel Foucault, *The Birth of the Clinic: An Archaeology of Medical Perception* [*Naissance de la clinique: une archéologie du regard médical*, 1963], translated by Alan Sheridan, Vintage Books / Random House (New York), 1973, p

273.
5 See Chapter 2, opening quotation and note 1.
6 W Boesiger and H Girsberger, *Le Corbusier 1910–65*, Les Éditions d'Architecture (Zurich), 1967, p 291.
7 *Ibid*.
8 Le Corbusier worked for Auguste Perret in Paris in 1908 at the age of 20, during his first trip away from his home town, La-Chaux-de-Fonds, Switzerland. See John Summerson, *The Classical Language of Architecture*, BBC (London) and MIT Press (Cambridge, MA), 1963, p 44.
9 See Jean-Louis Cohen (ed), *Le Corbusier: An Atlas of Modern Landscapes*, Museum of Modern Art (New York), 2013, p 203.
10 Boesiger and Girsberger, *Le Corbusier 1910–65*, p 291.
11 *Ibid*.
12 The metre was originally intended to be one ten-

millionth of the distance from the Earth's equator to the North Pole (at sea level): see the definition in the *Compact Oxford English Dictionary*, 2nd edition, Oxford University Press (Oxford), 1992.
13 Le Corbusier, *Une Maison – Un Palais*, Éditions Crès, 'Collection de 'L'Esprit Nouveau' (Paris), 1928, pp 22–3 (author's translation).
14 See Le Corbusier, *Towards a New Architecture* [*Vers une Architecture*, 1923], translated by Frederick Etchells, Dover Publications (New York), 1986, Chapter 3 on 'Regulating Lines', pp 69 and 78. The name 'Modulor' stems from Le Corbusier's notion of the 'module d'or'. It is derived from the Golden Section (0.618), a ratio where 'A to B' is the same as 'B to (A+B)'. The Golden Section (or Golden Ratio) is also embodied in the Fibonacci series: the sequential

addition of the two preceding numbers – 1, 1, 2, 3, 5, 8 ... ad infinitum. See also, Summerson, *The Classical Language of Architecture*, p 45.

15 See Introduction, note 5.

16 Rudolf Wittkower, *Architectural Principles in the Age of Humanism*, Alec Tiranti (London), 1952, p 13. See also Vitruvius, *The Ten Books on Architecture* [*De Architectura*, c 15 BC], translated by Morris Hicky Morgan, Dover Publications (New York), 1960, Book III, Chapter 1, i. See also Francesco di Giorgio Martini's Memorandum for S Francesco della Vigna (1535), translated by Giannantonio Moschini, *Guida per la Città di Venezia*, 1815, pp 55–61: 'And this mysterious harmony is such that when Plato in the Timaeus wished to describe the wonderful consonancy of the parts and fabric of the world, he took this as the first foundation of his description, multiplying as far as necessary these same proportions [...] until he had included the whole world and each of its members and parts.'

17 Leon Battista Alberti, *On The Art of Building in Ten Books* [*De Re Aedificatoria*, 1452], translated by Joseph Rykwert, Neal Leach and Robert Tavernor, Dover Publications (New York), 1987, Book Nine, Chapter 5. Alberti also defines beauty as 'that reasoned harmony of all the parts within a body, so that nothing may be added, taken away, or altered, but for the worse.' *On The Art of Building in Ten Books*, Book Six, Chapter 2.

18 Kurt Forster, 'Discussion: The Palazzo Rucellai and Questions of Typology in the Development of Renaissance Buildings', *Art Bulletin*, Vol 58, 1976, pp 109–13. Brenda Preyer, 'The Rucellai Palace', in FW Kent *et al*, *Giovanni Rucellai ed il suo Zibaldone: A Florentine Patrician and his Palace*, University of London (London), 1981, p 61.

19 A formal piazza was created between the medieval Palazzo del Senatore and the Palazzo dei Conservatori, both re-faced, and the Palazzo Nuovo built opposite to complete the composition.

20 Summerson, *The Classical Language of Architecture*, p 48.

21 For the first thesis of this book, regarding intermediary scale, see Chapter 1; for the second thesis of this book, regarding norms of scale, see Chapter 2; for the third thesis of this book, regarding patina, see Chapter 4; for the fourth thesis of this book, regarding touch, see Chapter 5.

7
On Scale and Detail

'The Parthenon has remained, torn apart but not jostled [...] If you look at the joints between the twenty sections of drums comprising the fluted columns, you won't find them, even by running a fingernail over these areas, which can only be differentiated by the slight irregularities in the patina that each marble has collected over time.'

Le Corbusier, *Journey to the East*, 1911[1]

Le Corbusier, with the fresh eyes of a 24-year-old, was not simply praising an extraordinary quality of craftsmanship when describing the grand flutes of the Parthenon's Doric columns, and their unimaginably fine joints. He was speaking of a complete experience of architecture; a moment of connection.[2] Jumping forward some forty years, to when the Chapel of Notre Dame du Haut at Ronchamp was on the drawing board in Le Corbusier's studio at Rue de Sèvres in Paris, we see a small exploratory model of the Ronchamp chapel, made of plaster of Paris; just cast, still soft.[3] Those same fingers which had caressed the stones of Athens, are recorded to this day in the model, gouging out the back of the wall and with a pencil, making rough holes in the smooth, curved front surface – the first physical experiments to perforate the chapel's

The Acropolis, Athens, 1911
Charles-Édouard Jeanneret [Le Corbusier] contemplating a broken Doric column during his 'journey to the East'.

thick south wall with small irregular openings, splaying to the interior and permeating it with light. For the maker and the viewer, the notion of 'touch' here underpins both the perception of architecture and the process of making it – sensually, intellectually and emotionally. It is irresistible to touch.

Within the Thickness of the Wall

Following Christopher Alexander's journey in *A Pattern Language*, from broad urban panoramas to the feelings in our fingertips, this final chapter zooms in to examine how scale matters in our experience of the city, in terms of what we find as we draw close to buildings, what they are made of and how they are put together. On the subject of 'Thick Walls', Alexander writes: 'Each house will have a memory; the characteristics and personalities of different individuals can be written in the thickness of the walls.'[4] He insists that 'walls must be at least a foot deep; perhaps even three of four feet deep' and observes that 'Window Places' – somewhere to sit or nestle by a window – are not a luxury but a basic human need, since we are 'drawn toward the light'.[5] He speaks of alcoves as a fundamental component of architecture – 'large rooms are not complete unless they have smaller rooms and alcoves opening off them'.[6] With echoes of John Summerson's table (discussed in the Introduction to this book), he talks about 'child caves', making the link between full size and 'miniature' scales in buildings. He examines details such

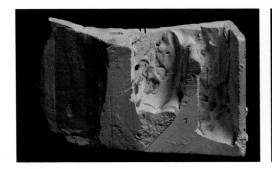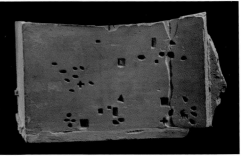

as how splayed reveals on the interior can sooth us by reducing glare and how it is natural for the edges of openings to be 'thickened', like our eyelids or lips. Of doorways, he writes: 'High doorways are simple and convenient. But a low door is often more profound'[7] – like the Arab *farqa* (literally meaning 'little hen'), the door within a door, found in traditional courtyard houses to ensure that a male visitor drops his head on entering, giving a moment for the ladies of the house to vanish before he raises it again.

Consistently throughout *A Pattern Language*, it is the threshold – the window, the door, the point or plane of overlap between inner and outer worlds – which establishes the pattern as part of a graded set of interconnected scales: 'every part of a town, a neighborhood, a building or a room is both an integral entity in itself, and joined to other entities to form a larger whole'.[8] Considering wall thickness at this point of overlap, there is no more lovely experience than sitting on the high cill of a window formed within the thick walls of a medieval castle, not only protected by its enclosure but part of something larger; a vast vaulted space inside, a piazza outside and the great mass of the building above.

As discussed in the previous chapter, the thick wall – the modelling of depth – is an invaluable part of scaling the city from the outside in as well as from the inside out. What we experience – what we touch, actually and metaphorically – is a factor of both how a wall is modelled, in space and volume, and how it is made, in texture and detail. As cities expand, and property moguls and construction companies develop ever-faster ways to build, there is a tendency for buildings to become lighter and thinner. There are even those who prefer disposable buildings to those which are meant to last, because it allows greater flexibility to redevelop in the future. But the thinning down of architecture is not a new problem. John Ruskin, in

Le Corbusier: working model of Ronchamp, 1953
Incisions made by hand in wet plaster become the basis of what is built.

Farqa: the 'little hen' door used in traditional Arab houses, Doha

The small door means that visitors look down as they come in, giving the ladies of the house time to move away into the most private areas.

his *Seven Lamps of Architecture* (1849), writes on 'The smallness of English Architecture': 'Until that street architecture of ours is bettered, until we give it some size and boldness, until we give our windows recess, and our walls thickness, I know not how we can blame our architects for their feebleness in more important work.'[9]

Ruskin's complaint in this instance was against the lightweight quality of the everyday vernacular, which he saw as undermining, both aesthetically and socially. In Ruskin's terms the single brick reveal (112 millimetres (4½ inches)), which has been typical of speculative housing development all over Britain since the 18th century, is not enough. It is interesting to see how the 19th-century workers' housing created by the Peabody Trust is distinctive because of its double-thickness reveals (225 millimetres (8¾ inches)), radically changing the feel of a development with little over 100 millimetres (4 inches) of brick. The St Andrews housing blocks at Bromley-by-Bow by Allies and Morrison, Maccreanor Lavington and Glenn Howells (2013) go one step further, using triple-depth reveals to create a 'larger than life' sense of solidity.[10] It is something which the majority of residents and passers-by will notice only subliminally. The value of the deep reveal however is not just its sense of robustness; the sense of being built to last (the very weight of the wall is affirmative). It is also the increased importance of shadows cast by the sun which, in combination with the softly striated brickwork and the shadows of the bold projecting balconies, bring the facade to life; raising the ordinariness of a well-built vernacular to something with a strong presence, seen from afar and close up. A balance is achieved between solidity, simplicity and richness.

Montepulciano and Todi: Muscle or Frill

So if, as designers, our goal is to seek a 'subliminal affirmative' – the tacit approval of the nine- or 90-year-old, the person on the street who is not educated in design but says 'It just has a good feel about it; I don't know why' – how do we go about it, in terms of detailing buildings? One answer is to achieve intensity by avoiding fuss; this is a matter of getting the scale right.

Montepulciano in Tuscany and Todi in Umbria both have domed pilgrimage churches below the town. Each one is in the form of a centralised Greek

Peabody housing, Roupell Street, London Waterloo, 1880s
Double brick reveals give a sense of solidity.

Allies and Morrison for
Barratt, St Andrews,
Bromley-by-Bow, 2013
Deep reveal detail, with
projecting balconies and
striped brickwork.

cross with multiple forms stepping down from the dome to the ground.
From a distance their relationship to the town above is similar; however, of
the two, it is San Biagio in Montepulciano, in honey-coloured local stone,
which particularly catches the eye as one draws close. The church, designed
by Antonio da Sangallo the Elder in the early 1500s, has detail which can
be read from a distance; it is solid and muscular, inside and out. By contrast
Santa Maria della Consolazione in Todi, designed by Cola da Caprarola

during the same period in a lighter limestone, although it is without doubt
a beautiful building, lacks the intermediary scale of detail so noticeable in
Sangallo's work; it is too fine; it lacks muscle.

Imagine Sangallo in conversation with his son and nephew, who worked
in his studio, urging them to hold off too much finesse in the drawings;

Antonio da Sangallo
the Elder, San Biagio,
Montepulciano, designed
1518, completed 1580
Robust details: an example
of 'intermediary scale'.

Cola da Caprarola, Santa
Maria della Consolazione,
Todi, begun 1508,
completed 1607
By comparison with San
Biagio, the details are fussy.

to remember the scale of the construction as a whole; 'it will be too far away; people will not read the detail; it will weaken the design'. Directing them not to view each motif as if it were close up – as the mason would carve it – but rather at some distance; or to think of a model – not too small but not too large – held in the hand; distance yourself like someone sitting in a pew, looking up, caressing the detail of the mighty dome above with your eyes.[11] The result is the larger-than-life rosettes of the vaults, set among plain white gypsum surfaces and the irresistible-to-touch, simple Ionic capitals, with their exaggerated volutes, which make this building, like all of Sangallo's work, so distinctive. It has scale. An example of a similar approach to scale in London today is the angled fins of the Blue Fin Building (2007) by Allies and Morrison, discussed and illustrated in Chapter 6.[12] From a distance they are rich in detail. Close up they are simple and solid, made of the largest single-depth extrusion (375 millimetres (14¾ inches)) which could be achieved at the time. Seen from within, the fins are very substantial, although they catch and reflect light, colour and shadow, and the viewer, like the fin, is part of a greater whole.

Antonio da Sangallo the Elder, Bishop's Palace, Montepulciano, 1580
Ionic capitals: simple solidity.

To an extreme degree, the works of Richard Rogers use muscularity – to
the point of super-scale – to surprise and engage us, working at a scale
which transcends the normal. The Centre Pompidou in Paris, completed
by Rogers with Renzo Piano in 1977, 're-scales' not only the surrounding

Antonio da Sangallo
the Elder, San Biagio,
Montepulciano, designed
1518, completed 1580
The rosettes of the internal
vaults have the quality of
being magnified: they have
been scaled to be read from
a distance.

Richard Rogers and Renzo
Piano, Centre Pompidou,
Paris, 1977
The titanic-scaled vent pipes
of the Centre Pompidou,
which mark out its
subterranean territory and
establish its zone of influence
beyond the main building,
have a transformational
quality. A grand urban piazza
becomes merely a surface
tracing, a manifestation of
something larger below.

urban context but the viewer too, whether
one is interacting with the building from
the street or becoming part of it from
inside the filigree of its gargantuan details.
Bearing in mind the size of the building –
an entire urban block – and the catalytic
role it had to play in the regeneration of
the Marais district (following its escape
from Le Corbusier's plans for wholesale
demolition),[13] it is a prime example, not
just of 'tuning up' the impact of such a
bold intervention in the historic city fabric
to the highest degree, but also of 'scaling
up' the detail, to achieve richness from
a distance; to bring the viewer closer; a
defining example of the mutuality of the
large and the small.

A recent example of muscle in Rogers's work is found at the building popularly dubbed 'the Cheesegrater' at 122 Leadenhall Street, in the City of London (2014), where the steel structure revealed at the base, opposite his Lloyd's Building (1986), creates a truly Piranesian atmosphere. This is sharply in contrast to the 'spindly legs' of Piano's Shard (2013), or his buildings at Central St Giles (2010), also in London, which feel so thin they might snap.

Rogers Stirk Harbour + Partners, 122 Leadenhall Street, London, 2014
The structure at the base of the building dubbed the 'Cheesegrater' has a Piranesian muscularity.

Venice, Rome and Doha

In the office of Allies and Morrison, where I learnt my trade, there was much talk of Venice and Rome. Venice was used as our paradigm of finesse: delicate tracery, consistent with the intimacy of its urban fabric; and Rome, the city of solidity and grandeur, was our exemplar of robustness. Venice, much loved by Ruskin, teaches us countless essential lessons in beauty. Nonetheless, with a focus on scale, this book tends towards the Roman, in the footsteps of Sangallo. Finesse and robustness are not, however, contradictory, as can be seen in the richness of the striped polychrome

Renzo Piano, The Shard,
London, 2013
The 'legs' of the Shard seem
very thin in proportion to
its bulk.

brickwork of St Andrews, Bromley-by-Bow, or the stonework of the Amiri
Diwan buildings that are currently under construction in Doha (already
discussed in Chapter 5).[13] The most straightforward of junctions are pursued
down to the last detail. The stone from Oman, hung on the concrete

frame, is only 40 millimetres (1½ inches) thick but at the corners, L-shaped stones are made of 150-millimetre (6-inch) thickness, to achieve a detail in scale with the stature of the work as a whole. Even the troublesome 9-millimetre (⅜-inch) silicone joints – always a second best in the architect's mind to 6-millimetre (¼-inch) grout-filled joints – become a moment of tactile delight; fine granules of stone are ground into the silicone while wet, creating their own micro-patina, to be felt at the scale of a finger and thumb.

Doge's Palace, Venice, from 1172
Delicate tracery characterises the city.

Castel Sant'Angelo, Rome, AD 130
Robust solidity, typical of Roman architecture.

Allies and Morrison, Amiri
Diwan Quarter, Doha, for
Msheireb, 2014
The 150-millimetre (6-inch)
stone return gives a sense of
solidity throughout.

Allies and Morrison, Amiri
Diwan Quarter, Doha, for
Msheireb, 2014
Stone granules pressed
into the silicone joints give
the surface of a man-made
chemical material, a natural
and tactile feel.

Ornament also plays its part. Robust simplicity is offset at moments of focus,
such as the 'VVIP porte cochere' of the Diwan Annex, by rich narrative-
laden pattern – hand-traced from photographs (local coral, cracked varnish,
ancient carvings); transformed and reprocessed by computers; tesselated,

pixellated, rasterised, vectorised and bound together into splines and closed shapes; tuned to refine solid to void ratios, corner terminations and the relationships between thicks and thins; sent to a stonemason with a five-axis CNC machine, or a metalworker with a waterjet; worked over by machines and finished by many hands, among gallons of water to keep the blades from burning; and finally brought to site and fixed in place. The richness of both process and product is latent, and apparent, in this work, held within a framework of craftsmanship and personal sensation. Inner layers are elaborated and revealed, singing out from a prevailing plainness in the facades and the surrounding context.

A pleasing detail is to be found in the nearby National Archive: the abstracted calligraphy of the main entrance. The deep-cut overlaid letters enrich the inner surfaces of the *madkhal* (porch) and fold round the corners

Allies and Morrison, Diwan Annex, Doha, for Msheireb, 2014
Narrative patterns find their provenance in Qatari motifs, in this case in the varnish of a traditional door, traced and transformed into contemporary ornament, adding enrichment to the timeless simplicity of the main structures.

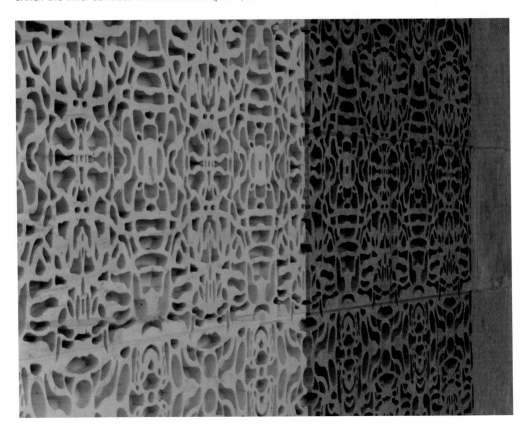

Allies and Morrison, Qatar National Archive, Doha, for Msheireb, 2014
Abstracted carved calligraphy, CNC cut in Omani limestone, invites the viewer to touch.

to address the grand portico. Even before the building is finished, the corner is becoming burnished by people touching it as they pass. It is literally irresistible. The theme of abstracted calligraphy runs through the Archive and serves as connector both of scales and of content. Handwritten, enlarged and inscribed, this is the human hand working at super-scale. It prompts the moment when we notice, pause, touch and remember a detail; it may be part of a grand design, it may be accidental but it is an important moment of connection. Our everyday experience of hurrying past, eyes to the ground, earphones plugged in, is transcended from time to time; we stop to absorb fully what is around us and our lives are the better for it.

Returning to Christopher Alexander, he describes the purpose of ornament as being 'to make the world more whole by knitting it together'.[14] In one of the last sections of his book, he draws an analogy between our physical environment and a Persian carpet: 'each part acts as figure and as boundary, at several levels'. He discusses interconnectedness and the graded 'range of scales' where ornament sits between the large scale of cities and buildings and the granular scale of nature and materials: 'there is an intermediate range of scales, a twilight zone, where [...] ornament fills the gap'.[15] This is not only a factor of how we experience scale in cities; we 'touch' things from far off with our eyes and our imaginations, and touch them again with our bodies when we are close. It is also a factor of narrative – the stories which buildings tell, inviting us to hear, and feed them too.

Like Nature

Materials are by nature sensuous. On approaching Louis Kahn's Salk Institute in La Jolla, California (1965), Juhani Pallasmaa 'felt immediately compelled to walk to the nearest concrete wall surface and sense its temperature; the suggestion of silk and live skin was overpowering'.[16] When considering the wall, Christopher Alexander writes 'a very good material is soft white gypsum plaster. It is warm in colour (even though white), warm to the touch […] and makes a mellow sound'.[17] The sounds and smells of materials, as well as their touch, are part of the art and the appreciation of architecture. This is our palette: how things look when they are new – textured, polished, tinted, seen in combination – and also when they are worn by time.

There is no space in the final pages of this book to examine the patina of the bronze of the Diwan Annex doors; what chemicals were used? How have they changed over time and been polished by use? However, it is worth pausing for a moment to ponder the fossils found in Portland stone,[18] quarried from Dorset for the majority of London's banks, offices and monuments, or the seashells found in the early concrete blocks of Old Doha: the intrinsic substance of materials revealed by years of weathering.[19] These have not been designed like the carvings of the Annex; they have just happened, but they are nonetheless essential to the touch and feel of the city. Judgements about materials – patina in the most microscopic sense of the word – are essential to the designer's work. They cannot be captured in drawings, models and specifications; mock-ups are needed at full scale.

Fossils in Portland stone, Chiswick Bridge, London, 1933
A millennia-old geology is revealed through weathering.

Sabban concrete, Doha
2014
Early concrete in Doha
was made from seashells
(*sabban*). As the material
weathers, the shells are
revealed.

The character of cities relies so much on details such as these, whether man-made or natural, and in some cases accidental. Even the shrapnel scars on bomb-blasted walls, saved as a memorial to a moment in time, are part of their nature. They are like the wrinkles on an ageing face. Indeed the view of the city as an organism, subject to natural processes, is nothing new. There is an important aspect of scale and detail which could have been mentioned in Chapter 4 on the subject of 'grain', but also belongs here. That is the role which ephemera – the accidental and undesigned – plays in our experience of the city. So much of our contact with cities happens at ground level. We do of course see cities from a distance – a skyline shimmering across a bay, a panorama hurtling past the window of a train or a teeming streetscape below seen from a skyscraper – but most of the time, we are on the street, among the confusion, meeting it face to face.

All aspects of design in our surroundings make a difference, both to designers and to non-designers, and all of us are appreciative of order of one kind or another. However, an experience such as exploring the shopping streets of Mongkok in Hong Kong or the Passage des Panoramas in Paris – the French capital's oldest shopping arcade, built in 1800 – is a case where richness of detail is intensified by the very fact that it is unplanned. Robert Venturi, Denise Scott Brown and Steven Izenour's wise words reminded the purist world of the value of impurism: 'The main justification for honky-tonk

Bomb damage to the Victoria and Albert Museum, Exhibition Road, London
Our encounters with buildings close up reveal details, both planned and accidental, which become part of a 'narrative connection' between ourselves and the world around us. Here, evidence of World War Two bombings on a section of the facade designed by Aston Webb (1909).

elements in architectural order is their very existence. They are what we have. Architects can bemoan or try to ignore them or even try to abolish them, but they will not go away.'[20] The coruscating chaos of multiple shop signs, projecting out over the street, with a thousand shapes, colours, logos, fonts and fixings is a rich filigree of the highest order. By its very randomness, scale is broken down to a fine grain, but at the same time combines into a collective spirit or a vernacular wholeness – at least for a particular street or neighbourhood – which mediates between the scale of the city and that of the individual.

Our encounters with detail of this sort are loaded with content, association and memories just as much as they are with aesthetic and practical interaction. Whether it is a multiplicity of shop signs seen in perspective or retail displays spilling out onto the street, or a self-seeded tree which has become a gathering place for old men to sit in the shade, it is at street level, and with the everyday, that we 'touch the city' in a most basic sense. It is perhaps in looking at Nature, and how we relate to her, that we find a clue to the connecting thread which runs through this book, sometimes apparent and sometimes latent.

A street in Mongkok, Hong Kong
Free-for-all retail signage makes the street tingle with detail.

When we remember that the roots of a tree, or the capillaries in our fingers, follow similar patterns to the flows of a river delta or a glacier, we are reminded of the interconnectedness of scales. Similarly the 'natural model' for how cities, spaces and buildings evolve over time, down to

Passage des Panoramas, Paris
Opened in 1800 and remodelled in the 1830s, this early shopping arcade displays a harmony of unplanned signage: the detail of the street at its best.

the last detail, is something to acknowledge and cherish. As Christopher Alexander argued: 'These patterns can never be "designed" or "built" in one fell swoop – but patient piecemeal growth, designed in such a way that every individual act is always helping to create or generate these larger global patterns, will, slowly and surely, over the years, make a community that has these global patterns in it.'[21]

References

1 Le Corbusier, *Journey to the East* [*Voyage d'Orient*, 1911], edited and translated by Ivan Žaknić with Nicole Pertuiset, MIT Press (Cambridge, MA and London), 1987, p 231.
2 *Ibid*. Le Corbusier continues: 'The base of the shaft, carved with twenty-four flutes, is as untarnished as the admiration you derive from it. The slab, chiseled all around like a bowl, reveals a difference in level of two or maybe three millimetres. This subtle detail executed two thousand years ago – a halo marking the base – is still perceptible, and as fresh and flawless as if the sculptor had only yesterday carried away the hammer and chisel that shaped his marble.'
3 This model is in the private collection of Niall Hobhouse.
4 Christopher Alexander, Sara Ishikawa, Murray Silverstein, Max Jacobson, Ingrid Fiksdahl-King and Shlomo Angel, *A Pattern Language: Towns, Buildings, Construction*, Oxford University Press (New York), 1977, p 911.
5 *Ibid* p 834.

6 *Ibid* p 829.
7 *Ibid* pp 1057, 1060 and 928.
8 *Ibid* p 1147.
9 John Ruskin, *The Seven Lamps of Architecture*, Chapter III, section 24, quoted in Kenneth Clark, *Ruskin Today*, John Murray (London), 1964, p 244.
10 See Chapter 4, section on 'History Speeded Up' and note 12.
11 The dome of S Biagio has a perfect echo – go to the centre and clap. E Barcucci, *Il Tempio di San Biagio a Montepulciano*, Le Balze (Montepulciano), 2000.
12 See Chapter 6, section on 'Skin and Bones'.
13 See Chapter 2, section on 'Paris 1925'.
13 See Chapter 5, section on 'Responsive Form'.
14 Alexander *et al.*, *A Pattern Language*, p 1149.
15 *Ibid*.
16 Juhani Pallasmaa, *The Thinking Hand*, John Wiley & Sons (Chichester), 2009, p 103. He continues: 'Kahn actually sought the grey softness of "the wings of a

moth" and added volcanic ash to the concrete mix in order to achieve this extraordinary inviting matt softness.'
17 Alexander *et al.*, *A Pattern Language*, p 1097, on 'Soft Inside Walls'.
18 A white Jurassic limestone, full of fossilised seashells. Portland stone has been used for buildings in the City of London and also widely abroad, including the United Nations Building in New York.
19 The early concrete blocks in Qatar were made with shells – *sabban* – the most readily available form of aggregate.
20 Robert Venturi, Denise Scott-Brown and Steven Izenour, *Learning from Las Vegas*, MIT Press (Cambridge, MA and London), 1972, p 121. On the same page, the authors observe: 'The seemingly chaotic juxtapositions of honky-tonk elements express an intriguing kind of vitality and validity, and they produce an unexpected approach to unity as well.'
21 Alexander *et al.*, *A Pattern Language*, p xix.

Conclusion

From Nature

'[…] when you build a thing you cannot merely build that thing in isolation, but must also repair the world around it and within it, so that the larger world at that one place becomes more coherent, and more whole; and the thing which you make takes its place in the web of nature as you make it.'

Christopher Alexander, *A Pattern Language*, 1977[1]

If we look very closely at our fingers, we find the familiar pattern of friction ridges, spiralling in towards the centre, towards the tip; it is a place of almost electrical sensitivity. Zoom out and we are reminded again that all scales are interconnected – by the same patterns found in shells and ferns, in whirlpools and tornadoes, and in the image of our solar system seen from outer space.

If one objective of this book is to talk about connections between people and places, and also to discuss connections between experiences – large and small, near and far, fast and slow – and scale-connections between

Fingerprint spiral
The connectedness of patterns from the microscopic to the macroscopic is the key to the relative nature of scale. Small: viewed close up, the spiral is revealed.

Whirlpool spiral
Medium: a spiral at the scale of the world we inhabit; something we can see close up or far away.

the patterns of Nature and the man-made world, then another, although perhaps more latent than overt within the text, is to think about beauty. Remembering Alberti's definition of beauty as the harmony between elements of varying scales, Nature is the key; 'Neither in the whole body nor in its parts does *concinnitas* flourish as much as it does in Nature herself; thus I might call it the spouse and soul of reason.'[2]

In the seven chapters of the book, we have zoomed from the sizing and scaling of cities, both as they are laid out by designers and as they naturally grow and shrink over time, to spaces within cities, then to the physical stuff of which those spaces are made and to the details which are revealed as we draw closer. Running throughout this journey is the theme of tactility. The tactile is both literal and metaphoric. It does indeed mean the warmth of south-facing stone steps on a sunny spring day or the naturally cooled air found in the shade of a tree by a lake in a park, and it applies to sound, smell and memory too – all that is around and inside us. It also applies, however, to those aspects of our urban environment which are not literally tangible; how do we 'touch' an urban space?

The notion of touch applies to the world which exists but it also applies to the world which does not yet exist: the world in our mind's eye, in the minds of designers and of all people who imagine things different from (and hopefully better than) the way they are. Designers are taught to be rational and all of us, whatever our education, have intellect, common sense, logic and other useful tools under the banner of 'reason' at our disposal. But what did Alberti mean by the word 'reason'? He meant something more complex: a thought process guided by – stemming from – the harmony which he found in Nature. Cities are man-made but we only have to look at slow-grown, unplanned street patterns to realise that they are natural too: as natural as the growth of a coral reef, or as water finding its way from source to sea. So to what extent do designers and appreciators of cities learn from Nature, and to what extent is their reason guided by things beyond their own intellect? Not enough. Indeed,

Solar system spiral
Large: a spiral so large we cannot see it except by means of satellites; something beyond our physical experience.

'reason' in its fullest form is the fusion – the interweaving, balancing or coexistence – of both intellect and intuition; by which we can participate as creative beings in the 'web of Nature'.

Our ability to receive or connect with the world around us to the full – at any scale – is balanced by our ability to project our thoughts into the world, beyond what already exists. In the preceding pages we have examined our experience of and interaction with the city, its past and its future, at all scales. This is a question of both consciousness and unconsciousness. City life is hard work; it can be harsh. The noise and movement, the accelerating speed, the numbers of choices can all be exhausting. A successful city, however, is one where people feel at home. With Christopher Alexander, Alberti and many others as our guides, our ability to transcend the hurly-burly will be a lifeline; to find a place – to make a place – in the city, for ourselves and our fellow human beings to touch and be touched, to make scale-connections between things, will be one of the keys to that success.

All Change

Our experience of cities, and the role they play in our lives, is changing fast. As evolving beings in an evolving environment, it is impossible to assess how significantly the digital age, which is still in its infancy, will change us. It is a paradox that our fingertips – the most sensitive of places – should be so important to two aspects of our lives which may be in conflict: touch (in the broad sense of the word) and touch-screen technology (along with all virtual experience). To be able to communicate with any part of the world from literally any place at minimal cost is something quite new, as is the ubiquitous access we have to infinite quantities of information. It is a new experience of placelessness. It is a wonderful liberation but perhaps also a new kind of bondage.

What concerns this book, though, is not so much the issue of freedom as that of touch: the very real danger that our fingertips, metaphorically speaking, are being desensitised. To be looking at a smartphone rather than the world around us or into each other's eyes; to prefer to text than to speak; to stay indoors with a screen rather than go out in the street, and even then to hear the world through headphones; it is as if between us and the city we inhabit, a 'layer of insulation' is developing, a kind of protective coating – but protection against what? It is like callouses on our fingers; a spreading numbness. Are people less surprised than they used to be? Is there less awe in the lives of the young ('I don't need to go there, I've seen it on the Internet')? Even in terms of designing and making, to draw on a glass screen rather than making marks with graphite or chalk on paper has a homogenising quality; it may open up possibilities but it takes away textures, smells and dust; it is a loss of flavour. As we zoom, faster and faster – closer in and further away – there is a real danger that while the Pandora's box of the digital world gives us more than we have been used to in the past – more knowledge, more choices, more ways to spend time – yet we have less; less contact with the world around us. Too many truffles; not enough taste.

So what has this to do with scale? It is not so much a matter of our physical environment, but it will increasingly affect how we relate to it. In as far as this book has suggested that 'scale' is the perception of size and our ability to make interconnected, graded connections between ourselves and places – like sequential patterns in the 'web of Nature' – the danger is that this process will be literally flattened by the touch screen, by dulling our sensitivity or, even worse, our creativity. There is no certainty that our tangible relationship with the city in the future, as the digital age increasingly permeates our lives, will be better or worse than in the past, but what is for sure is that it will be very different and we are only at the very beginnings of that change. Our evolution through this new age of communication, where time and space are to some extent being redefined, will run its course over the coming centuries, and this book will not change that. However, it is important here to emphasise the value of 'touch' at all scales, reminding ourselves that scale matters and is tactile; even at the scale of the city, it is within our grasp. It is the purpose of this book to ask makers and appreciators of cities to savour and enhance the connection between people and places – to promote 'placefulness' – even though we are now able to be in a hundred places all at once with less regard to the physical than we had before. It is to ask designers and users of cities to acknowledge that the smallness of the individual and the largeness of the city are by nature connected, and with this in mind, to step forward with a spirit of responsibility and a sense of belonging.

Reprise

'Touch' was the fourth of our theses. Before closing, it is worth recapping the other three. 'Patina' was the third – observing that grains and textures found in old things (slow-grown) can teach us lessons about scale which can be applied even when time or the process of development is 'speeded up' by the demands of economics, greed or impatience. The importance of patina applies at all scales: city planning, street-making, the selection of materials and the honing of detail. The second thesis was that of 'normative absolutes': that although scale is relative, human scale is more or less a constant, providing a datum or grading device by which we can measure all scales, both static and dynamic. Our bodies are indeed a measure – the measure – of the world around us, enabling us to perceive proportional relationships between one thing and another; the touchstone of our experience. The first thesis was about 'intermediary scale': a necessity in successful cities, to bridge between scales; big but not too big; fine but not too fine, and to ensure a connection between sensations from afar and close up.

These theses are brought together in the notion of the child and the giant in us all. We interact with the world, not only at our own scale but as a child, in search of grandeur, and also as a giant, craving intimacy. This is not the voice of a 'middle way' – promoting a compromise somewhere between large and small, robust and fine. Rather it is calling for parallel perceptions – layers of largeness and smallness to be overlaid, from the scale of the city, to the scale of the detail. This is in the nature of being human, although it is only through metaphor that it can be fully explained. In Bachelard's words, 'one must go beyond logic to experience what is large in what is small'.[3]

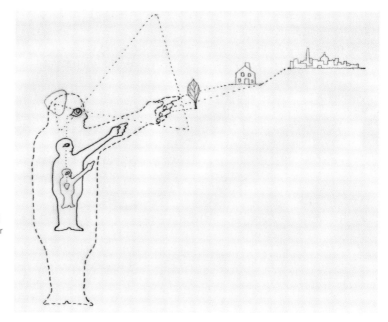

Inner and outer, near and far: drawing by the author, 2014

We see and touch the world with our bodies and with our imaginations; our feelings and our sensations work at both these levels. In terms of scale, perceptions large and small, experiences near and far – they coexist. This is part of the beauty of life.

Epilogue

It is six o'clock in the morning; it is dark. I have just woken up and I look out of the window. Far below me I see a shape, black as night: Regent's Park. We are flying over London. There is King's Cross: great linear shapes of the Goods Yard to the north, converging lines between the two stations to the south. The masterplan of new blocks, streets and squares – my life for five years – is emerging. By night it is the cranes, flashing lights, coruscating like stars in a moonless sky, which catch the eye. The sinuous line of the canal is invisible to my bleary gaze.

We are over the Olympic Park; we wheel southwards. The stadium glows but the River Lea is no more than an inky line, winding its way down to the Thames. St Andrews, Bromley-by-Bow can just be discerned as an array of dots: vertical dots of light denote the tower; grids of horizontal dots, repeating shapes, indicate the trio of urban blocks.

Canary Wharf and the City beyond look close to each other; centre and edge are compounded. We wheel again and the Shard appears as an eruption of glass, with dark railway lines gorging into its base.

Bankside is below me: more glistening lights, cranes, scaffold, hoardings; construction sites are waking up. The city is changing. Beyond it, beyond the City of London, the road to Colchester can be seen, running straight, as far as the eye can see; this is the road which Boadicea travelled in AD 60 in her chariot, on her way to take London.

The Millennium Wheel is in blue, lights circling round and round. Beyond it, shining out from the maze, is Piccadilly Circus – the focal point of this animated panorama. I zoom in. My view is suddenly very vivid: advertisements for TDK, Hyundai and Coca-Cola flicker, all clearly visible in miniature. This is the wall of advertising, retained in preference to rooms with views, not because it is part of our national identity or essential to 'brand London', but simply because it is more lucrative than renting the spaces behind as offices or apartments.

We fly on over the parks and the winding river. The villages of west London are delineated in a combination of sickly orange and cool white. Low-energy LEDs are taking over, making the orange glow of London a thing of the past.

Piccadilly Circus, London
See from a plane or up close, the city draws us in: into its fabric of buildings and spaces, of people, activity and communication.

We are momentarily over the house where I grew up, and the house where I live now – my family will still be asleep. Over Kew Gardens and the Stone Pine; we are getting closer; we are coming in to land.

References

1 Christopher Alexander, Sara Ishikawa, Murray Silverstein, Max Jacobson, Ingrid Fiksdahl-King and Shlomo Angel, *A Pattern Language: Towns, Buildings, Construction*, Oxford University Press (New York), 1977, p xiii.
2 Leon Battista Alberti, *On The Art of Building in Ten Books* [*De Re Aedificatoria*, 1452], translated by Joseph Rykwert, Neal Leach and Robert Tavernor, Dover Publications (New York), 1987, Book Nine, Chapter 5.
3 Gaston Bachelard, *The Poetics of Space* [*La Poétique de l'espace*, 1957], translated by Maria Jolas, Beacon Press (Boston, MA), 1969, p 150.

Select Bibliography

Abdullah, Mohammad Ali, *Patterns in Gulf Architecture*, National Council for Culture, Arts and Heritage (Doha), 2002

Adler, Gerald, Brittain-Catlin, Timothy and Fontana-Giusti, Gordana (eds), *Scale: Imagination, Perception and Practice in Architecture*, Routledge (New York), 2012

Alberti, Leon Battista, *On the Art of Building in Ten Books* [*De Re Aedificatoria*, 1452], translated by Joseph Rykwert, Neal Leach and Robert Tavernor, Dover Publications (New York), 1987

Alexander, Christopher, Ishikawa, Sara, Silverstein, Murray, Jacobson, Max, Fiksdahl-King, Ingrid and Angel, Shlomo, *A Pattern Language: Towns, Buildings, Construction*, Oxford University Press (New York), 1977

Alexander, Christopher, *The Timeless Way of Being*, Oxford University Press (New York), 1979

Anonymous, *Le Corbusier: Architect of the Century*, Arts Council of Great Britain (London), 1987

Bachelard, Gaston, *The Poetics of Space* [*La Poétique de l'espace*, 1957], translated by Maria Jolas, Beacon Press (Boston, MA), 1969

Benevolo, Leonardo, *The History of the City*, Scolar Press (London), 1980

Boesiger, W and Girsberger, H, *Le Corbusier 1910–65*, Les Éditions d'Architecture (Zurich), 1967

de Botton, Alain, *The Architecture of Happiness*, Penguin Books (London), 2007

Campbell, Kelvin, *Massive Small*, Urban Exchange (London), 2011

Carmona, Matthew, Tiesdell, Steve, Heath, Tim and Oc, Taner, *Public Places – Urban Spaces: The Dimensions of Urban Design*, Routledge (London), 2003

Chipperfield, David, *Form Matters*, Walther König (Cologne), 2009

Clark, Kenneth, *Ruskin Today*, John Murray (London), 1964

Cohen, Jean-Louis (ed), *Le Corbusier: An Atlas of Modern Landscapes*,

Museum of Modern Art (New York), 2013

Cullen, Gordon, *The Concise Townscape*, Architectural Press (London), 1961

Curtis, William JR, *Modern Architecture Since 1900*, Phaidon (Oxford), 1982

Farrell, Terry, *The City as a Tangled Bank: Urban Design vs Urban Evolution*, AD Primers series, John Wiley & Sons (Chichester), 2014

Farrell, Terry, *Interiors and the Legacy of Postmodernism*, Laurence King (London), 2011 – includes an essay by Tim Makower entitled 'Postmodernism and the rebirth of architectural storytelling'

Firsht, Elana, '"Assembly Line Americanisation": Henry Ford's Progressive Politics', *Michigan Journal of History*, Fall 2012

Frampton, Kenneth, *Modern Architecture: A Critical History*, Thames & Hudson (London), 1980

Gehl, Jan, *Cities for People*, Island Press (Washington, DC; Covelo, CA; and London), 2010

Gibberd, Frederick, *Town Design*, Architectural Press (London), 1953

Glaeser, Edward, *Triumph of the City*, Pan Macmillan (London), 2011

Gombrich, EH, *Art and Illusion*, Phaidon (London), 1977

Gombrich, EH, *Meditations on a Hobby Horse*, Phaidon (London), 1963

Herron, Jerry, 'The Last Pedestrians', *Places*, Design Observer Group, 4 October 2012

Hoag, John D, *Islamic Architecture*, Electa (Milan), 1975; Faber and Faber (London), 1987

Hollis, Edward, *The Secret Lives of Buildings: From the Parthenon to the Vegas Strip in Thirteen Stories*, Portobello (London), 2009

Jacobs, Jane, *The Death and Life of Great American Cities*, Random House (New York), 1961; Vintage Books (New York), 1992

Jaidah, Ibrahim Mohamed and Bourennane, Malika, *The History of Qatari Architecture 1800–1950*, Skira (Milan), 2009

Jencks, Charles, *Post-Modernism*, Rizzoli (New York), 1987

Jung, CG, 'Mind and the Earth' [part of 'Die Erdbedingtheit der Psyche', 1927], *Contributions to Analytical Psychology*, 1928, Read Books (London), 2008

Kasarda, John D and Lindsay, Greg, *The Evolution of Airport Cities and the Aerotropolis*, Insight Media (London), 2008

Al-Kholaifi, Mohammad Jassim, *The Traditional Architecture in Qatar*, National Council for Culture, Arts and Heritage (Doha), 2006

Koolhaas, Rem and Mau, Bruce, *S, M, L, XL*, Monacelli Press (New York), 1995

Koolhaas, Rem, *Delirious New York*, Monacelli Press (New York), 1978

Kostof, Spiro, *The City Shaped: Urban Patterns and Meanings through History*, Thames & Hudson (London), 1991

Krier, Leon, *Urban Space* [*Stadtraum in Theorie und Praxis*, 1975], translated by Christine Czechowski and George Black, Academy Editions (London), 1979

Le Corbusier, *Towards a New Architecture* [*Vers une Architecture*, 1923], translated by Frederick Etchells, Dover Publications (New York), 1986

Le Corbusier, *The City of To-morrow and its Planning* [*Urbanisme* [1924], 8th edition, 1929], translated by Frederick Etchells, Dover Publications (New York), 1987

Le Corbusier, *Journey to the East* [*Voyage d'Orient*, 1911], edited and translated by Ivan Žaknić with Nicole Pertuiset, MIT Press (Cambridge, MA and London), 1987

Lynch, Kevin, *The Image of the City*, MIT Press (Cambridge, MA and London), 1960

MacDonald, William L, *The Architecture of the Roman Empire: An Introductory Study*, Yale University Press (New Haven, CT and London), 1982

Marchand, Yves and Meffre, Romain, *The Ruins of Detroit*, with essays by Thomas J Sugrue and Robert Polidori, Steidl (Göttingen) and Thames & Hudson (London), 2010

Martienssen, RD, *The Idea of Space in Greek Architecture*, Witwatersrand University Press (Johannesburg), 1956

Morris, William, *News from Nowhere* [1876], Penguin Books (Harmondsworth), 1962

Morrison, Philip and Phylis, and the Office of Charles and Ray Eames, *Powers of Ten: About the Relative Size of Things in the Universe*, Scientific American Library (New York), 1982

Pallasmaa, Juhani, *The Thinking Hand: Existential and Embodied Wisdom in Architecture*, AD Primers series, John Wiley & Sons (Chichester), 2009

Pevsner, Nikolaus and Cherry, Bridget, *The Buildings of England, London 1: The Cities of London and Westminster*, Penguin Books (Harmondsworth), 1957

Picon, Antoine, *Ornament: The Politics of Architecture and Subjectivity*, AD Primers series, John Wiley & Sons (Chichester), 2013

Psarra, Sophia, Kickert, Conrad and Pluviano, Amanda, 'Paradigm Lost: Industrial and post-industrial Detroit – An analysis of the street network and its social and economic dimensions from 1796 to the present', *Urban Design International*, Vol 18, No 4, 2013, pp 257–81

Rowe, Colin and Koetter, Fred, *Collage City*, MIT Press (Cambridge, MA), 1978

Rykwert, Joseph, *The Idea of a Town*, Faber and Faber (London), 1976

Scott, Geoffrey, *The Architecture of Humanism*, Constable & Co (London), 1914

Scott Brown, Denise, *Having Words*, Architectural Association (London), 2009

Sebald, WG, *The Rings of Saturn* [*Die Ringe des Saturn*, 1995], Random House (London), 2002

Self, Will, *Psychogeography*, Bloomsbury (London), 2007

Sennett, Richard, *Flesh and Stone: The Body and the City in Western Civilization*, WW Norton (New York), 1996

Serlio, Sebastiano, *The Five Books of Architecture* [1554], reprint of the English edition of 1611, Dover (New York), 1982

Summerson, John, *The Classical Language of Architecture*, BBC (London) and MIT Press (Cambridge, MA), 1963

Summerson, John, *Georgian London*, Pleiades Books (London), 1945

Summerson, John, *Heavenly Mansions [and other essays on architecture]* [1949], WW Norton (London and New York), 1998

Tavernor, Robert, *Smoot's Ear: The Measure of Humanity*, Yale University Press (New Haven, CT), 2007

Venturi, Robert, *Complexity and Contradiction in Architecture*, The Museum of Modern Art Papers on Architecture, Museum of Modern Art (New York), 1966

Venturi, Robert, Scott Brown, Denise and Izenour, Steven, *Learning from Las Vegas*, MIT Press (Cambridge, MA and London), 1972

Vitruvius, *The Ten Books on Architecture* [*De Architectura, c* 15 BC], translated by Morris Hicky Morgan, Dover Publications (New York), 1960

Ward-Perkins, John B, *Roman Architecture*, Faber and Faber (London) and Electa (Milan), 1974

Wittkower, Rudolf, *Architectural Principles in the Age of Humanism*, Alec Tiranti (London), 1952

Index

Figures in italics indicate captions

Picture Credits

The author and the publisher gratefully acknowledge the people who gave their permission to reproduce material in the book. While every effort has been made to contact copyright holders for their permission to reprint material the publishers would be grateful to hear from any copyright holder who is not acknowledged here and will undertake to rectify any errors or omissions in future editions.

Front cover image © Tim Makower

Images; p 8, 11, 12, 13, 14, 15, 16, 17, 18, 26, 27, 28, 32, 36, 37, 39, 40, 41, 42, 46, 47, 52, 53, 54, 56, 57, 58, 59, 61, 62, 65, 66, 67, 68, 78, 79, 80, 82, 83, 85, 86, 87, 91, 93, 94, 95, 96, 99, 103, 106, 107, 111, 112, 113 (t), 115, 116, 117, 120, 121, 123, 132, 133, 134, 136, 137, 138, 140, 142, 144, 145, 146, 147, 151, 152, 153, 157, 158, 159, 160, 161, 162, 163, 165, 167, 168, 169, 175, 181, 182, 183, 184, 185, 186, 187, 191, 192, 193, 194, 195, 196, 198, 205 © Tim Makower; p 20 © 2014 Eames Office, LLC; p 21 © Map data: Google, Bluesky; p 25 © Katharine Makower. From the collection of the author's family; p 29 © authentichistory. com; p 30 © From the Collections of The Henry Ford, www.thehenryford.org; p 31 © Walter P. Reuther Library, Archives of Labor and Urban Affairs, Wayne State University; p 34 © Bettmann/CORBIS, photo Philip Gendreau; p 38 © AFP/Getty Images, photo Jeff Kowaslky/ Stringer; p 48, 77, 139, 179 © FLC/ ADAGP, Paris and DACS, London 2014; p 60 © Tom Sly; p 63 © TfL from the London Transport Museum collection; p 69 © Allies and Morrison. All rights reserved; p 81 © Ana Gonzalez Laucirica; p 88 © The Centre for GIS – Ministry of Municipality & Urban Planning; p 92 © Paul Atkinson/Shutterstock; p 97, 102, 104, 108, 128, 188, 189 © Edward Denison, 2014; p 98 © Getty Images/Hulton Archive; p 101 © Garsya/Shutterstock; p 113 (b), 114 © West 8 urban design & landscape architecture; p 118 © Miller Hare courtesy of King's Cross Central Limited Partnership; p 122 © Jeremy Richards/ Shutterstock; p 129 © Alessandro Zocc/Shutterstock; p 131 Air photography by Hunting Aerosurveys Ltd (dissolved 2003); p 143 © Photo Gemma Levine. Reproduced by permission of the Henry Moore Foundation; p 148 © Ateliers Jean Nouvel & Artefactory; p 149 © Ateliers Jean Nouvel, Artefactory, TDIC, Louvre Abu Dhabi, plans for Louvre Abu Dhabi, 2008; p 150 © Ateliers Jean Nouvel, Artefactory, TDIC, Louvre Abu Dhabi, rendering for the Louvre Abu Dhabi, 2008; p 164 © Rene Burri / Magnum Photos; p 172 © Ivonne Wierink/ Shutterstock; p 173 © Pete Veale; p 174 © Max Fenton; p 180 © Niall Hobhouse: Private Collection; p 190 (t) © Dmitri Ometsinsky/Shutterstock, (b) © Marco Rubino/Shutterstock; p 197 © Guo Zhong Hua/Shutterstock; p 201 (l) © Africa Studio/Shutterstock, (r) © Elaine Davis/Shutterstock; p 202 Courtesy of NASA